The basic book of

VEGETABLE GROWING

The basic book of

VEGETABLE GROWING

W. E. Shewell-Cooper

Drake Publishers Inc. **New York**

Published in 1973 by
Drake Publishers Inc
381 Park Avenue South
New York, N.Y. 10016

© W. E. Shewell-Cooper, 1973

Library of Congress Cataloging in Publication Data
    The basic book of vegetable growing.
Shewell-Cooper, Wilfred Edward, 1900–

    1. Vegetable gardening.   I. Title
SB322.S463   635   73–3373

ISBN 0–87749–485–1

Printed in Great Britain

Illustrations

TO MY TWO SONS

Caerveth Ramsay George and Jeremy Gervase Edward

who, I hope, will enjoy this book

*An intercrop of
'butter head' lettuce
in between rows of
broad beans.*

1 Designing the Vegetable Garden

Whether long and narrow, wide and broad, three-quarters of an acre, or just a rod, your vegetable garden should be so designed that the rows of vegetables may be arranged to run north and south. When the rows have to run east and west, far more shadows are thrown, and as a result the crops are not so early and not, perhaps, so good. Those with small gardens appreciate short rows because they can then arrange to have a greater variety. When the rows are a good length, running north and south in a small area, obviously the numbers of rows are perforce curtailed. Under such conditions it is a nuisance to sow a quarter of a row of one variety and continue with a quarter row of another variety and so on.

The great mistake that beginners often make is to have the vegetable garden a mass of paths. Paths are necessary it is true, but, unless the area is a large one, one good path 4 ft wide is sufficient. If any other paths are necessary, these should be temporary ones, such as are made by just treading the soil down.

In the larger garden it will be possible to have a path all the way round. This was the usual custom in the large walled-in gardens attached to old mansions. The advantage of such a system is that narrow borders are formed around the outside, and in this way north, south, east and west borders come in for special treatment.

The south border will be the warmest of all, and is generally used for the early crops. It tends to be on the dry side, and so has to receive copious waterings. If there is a fence or wall at the back of it, this is useful for growing dessert plums, or even apricots or peaches. The east border is suitable for permanent crops like seakale, rhubarb, and globe artichokes. Such crops as the perennial spinach may also be grown there. The north border, being the most shady, can be used for late crops – for marrows, kohlrabi, and so on. These narrow borders are useful because they enable very short rows of special crops to be grown, and gardeners who are fond of unusual vegetables will find the south and north borders just wide enough for the few rows to be grown. The west border can be used for a seed bed or for frames.

In the smaller garden the path need only go down one side. In this case the seedbeds must be in between the rows of other vegetables, and fitted in as space allowed. It was

Laying down a path, using a spirit level to make sure that the path is level.

only possible to cater for a three-course rotation, and a very narrow pathway was allowed for on the east side.

Paths may be made with cinders, gravel, crazy paving, or concrete. The crazy paving or flag path is not quite in keeping with vegetables. The gravel or concrete path is more lasting and will stand the constant barrowing that has to be done. If the gravel path can be tarred or covered with one of the more modern bitumen compounds, so much the better, for it then becomes easier to keep clean, and there is less chance of taking portions of the path under one's boots on to the garden. This is one of the greatest disadvantages of the cinder path.

Whatever path is made, it must have a good foundation. It must be porous, so that excess moisture can flow away, and this porosity can be achieved by burying clinkers, old iron, flints and similar material 3 ft down. If the pathway can be excavated to this depth, all kinds of waste material can be buried. This can be covered with larger stones, and finally the gravel can be put in position. A 2-in layer of gravel is enough, and a ton of gravel will cover 18 square yards. The concrete path is perhaps the cleanest and most durable of all, and it should be laid on the same solid foundation.

Let the area be open, and do not muddle it with tall trees. A dwarf hedge, say of *Lonicera nitida,* will make an excellent division between the vegetable garden and the flower garden. There is nothing ugly in vegetables, especially when well-grown. The almost soldier-like rows and distances adopted, give an air of utility, but this does not mean that it is anything to be ashamed of.

2 Soils: their Care and Improvement

Soils contain inorganic clay, limestone and sand, plus organic vegetable and animal remains called 'humus'. The properties of the soil in our gardens depends on which of these is predominant.

Only those who have had a garden in different parts of the country really appreciate the extent to which a particular type of soil influences the growth of plants. The light gravels over chalk suffer from drought very quickly, and it is difficult to grow the best vegetable crops in these soils unless plenty of good compost is added. On the other hand, the light loams, rich in humus, that are of a good depth and have perfect drainage, can produce crops of show standard comparatively easily.

A **Clay Soil** Clay soil retains the moisture, but it is difficult to cultivate because of its heaviness, and it is apt to crack badly in the summer if it is allowed to dry out. During drought periods clay soils need hoeing constantly, and only mulches of good compost can prevent these fissures from appearing. Clay soils usually need draining. A vegetable garden with such a soil that is badly drained is almost impossible to work, and crops die out because of waterlogging. Lime is usually necessary because it prevents the particles from clogging together.

Clay soils may be improved by the addition of properly-made compost, spent hops, wool shoddy, or other similar organic material. Clay soils are generally rich in potash, but are frequently deficient in nitrogen.

A **Marly Soil** Marly soil is really a type of chalky clay. Where clay predominates it is called a *clay marl*, and where chalk predominates, it is known as *chalky marl*. Marls may contain between 5 per cent and 20 per cent of calcium carbonate.

A **Sandy Soil** Most people like a sandy soil because it is easy to work at any time of the year. It is not usually badly drained and so plants do not die in the winter through waterlogging. It is a soil that warms up quickly in the spring, and it usually produces earlier crops than clay soils for this reason. On the other hand, sandy soils dry out quickly in the summer, and so plants may suffer badly from drought. Such soils are very hungry and large quantities of properly-made compost should be applied each year. They need compost in order to retain moisture. Sedge peat may be applied where compost has not been made.

Sands are usually lacking in potash and phosphates, though they are high in silica. Sand has little retentive power for plant foods, so there is a steady loss of potash and nitrates in the drainage water.

A Peaty Soil In some areas peaty soils are found which consist largely of organic matter. These soils have been produced by the growth and decay of 'aquatic' plants over a very long period. Such soils may be badly waterlogged and so must be drained. They are usually deficient in lime. It may be necessary to apply lime every year on such soils at the rate of, say, 7 oz to the square yard.

Such soils are easy to work and need not have quantities of organic manure added to them. Organic fertilizers are quite suitable. There is no necessity to apply lots of nitrogen, but phosphates and potash are necessary.

A Loamy Soil Most people find difficulty in understanding what *loam* means. A loam is an ideal mixture of the three soils already mentioned. When clay, sand and properly-composted vegetable matter are mixed in the right proportions, a loam is produced. Loams are ideal because owing to the clay they contain, they do not dry out quickly. They do not 'pan down' hard like cement, because of the sand they contain. They are easily worked, highly productive and they support nearly all vegetable crops satisfactorily.

Soils with a preponderance of clay are known as *clayey loams*, and those containing more sand than clay, *sandy loams*. It should be the aim of all gardeners to turn their soil into a loam. This can be done by the addition of organic matter, and by efficient drainage. The ideal loam provides the roots of growing plants with a 'balance' of food, air and water – all necessary to sustain plant life.

SUBSOILS Subsoils play almost as important a part in the success of vegetable culture as do the actual soils. For instance, should the subsoil be chalk, then the drainage will be perfect, and chalk brought to the surface during deep cultivation (which I never recommend) will prevent the soil from becoming acid and will obviate the necessity of applying lime. Chalk itself is an unpleasant material to work in; therefore when cultivating on soils over chalk, care should be taken never to bring large quantities of the subsoil to the surface. During dry years the chalk acts as such a perfect 'drain' that the soil overlying it is dried out quickly and the crops suffer in consequence.

Should the subsoil be clay, then a barrier may be formed through which water cannot pass. This soon produces surface waterlogging. Such subsoils need draining. If the vegetable grower is to achieve success on a soil over such formation, he must break up that subsoil with an iron crowbar.

Draining Many gardens and allotments are already drained before the occupier takes them over. Sometimes these drains become blocked and a blocked drain is worse than no drain at all. It should be traced to its outlet, and, if it is found that the water is not running freely, the drain should be 'rodded' and cleaned.

The main function of the agricultural drain is to remove excess soil-water. Its effect is to allow the air to penetrate throughout the soil, and by the removal of excess moisture to make it possible for the soil to become warmer. Many plants will not grow satisfactorily on cold soils, and so the question of soil temperature is important. Experiments have shown that a drained soil may be 6 degrees F warmer than a similar undrained soil.

As a general rule, drains should not be deeper than 2 ft 6 ins and the drain pipes should not be more than 15ins apart; 3 in drain pipes are quite suitable for sub-mains, but 8 in drains at least should be used for the mains.

It is a good plan to cover agricultural drain pipes with clinkers or coarse brick rubbish, as this prevents the pipes from becoming sealed up. Drain pipes may be blocked by the roots of trees, grass and plants, and that is the reason they have to be examined if it is found that they are not working properly.

Where it is impossible to use drain pipes, large stones and clinkers may be buried 18 ins or 2 ft down to help carry the excess soil-water away. If a 4 in thickness of such stones can be buried 2 ft down and in strips 3 ft wide, it should be possible to carry the excess water down this home-made 'culvert' to the lowest point in the garden or to some ditch outside.

Digging After 10 whole years of research into rival no-digging versus digging practices, I came to the conclusion that it was far better to allow the worms to do their important tunnelling work undisturbed. Thus bastard trenching, true trenching and ridging, which I used to advise, became taboo.

The 'no-digging' plan is to cover the ground, even in heavy soils – in late autumn or early winter – with properly-made compost at least an inch deep. Then the worms start tunnelling up and down, pulling some of the compost into the ground, and enabling the millions of living organisms in the soil to work on it and convert it into the invaluable colloid or jelly, known as humus. The gardener simply mulches the soil with compost or sedge peat an inch deep, and the worms prepare the soil and do the necessary aeration and 'digging'.

Left all winter with its blanket covering of compost, the soil will be ready to be lightly forked in the spring, to incorporate the powdery compost an inch or so deep into it. There is then sufficient loose soil plus compost into which to sow seeds.

Single Digging All that is necessary is to dig up the 'spit', and invert it ahead of the work. Usually a shallow trench is dug out first and the soil taken to the other end of the plot; thus the surface of the soil is kept level all the way through. Single digging is generally done during spring or summer in order to prepare the soil for a particular crop, or after one crop has been harvested and before the next one is sown.

Spring Cultivations When the spring comes, the gardener needs to make the soil warm as early as he can. At this time of the year light forking and raking will produce the fine tilth required for seed-growing. Ideally the soil in a seed bed should be such that every particle is no larger than a grain of wheat.

The compost which has been applied in the autumn will be lightly forked in, and this will help to keep the moisture in the soil and also to prevent the annual weeds from growing. During the summer, hoeing is done occasionally to provide a *dust mulch* – a loose surface of dusty soil which prevents the evaporation of the soil moisture below. If the soil is firm right up to the surface, then the sun and wind are able to draw up the moisture and cause its evaporation. Compost on the surface of the soil prevents this.

Both the Dutch hoe and the draw hoe can play a part. Work can be done quickly with a Dutch hoe and as it is used whilst walking backwards, the gardener's footmarks are covered up. Hoeing must be carried out if and when weeds appear. (With the compost system, there are few

Earthing up celery

weeds.) Many crops need an extra mulching with an organic material. Peas and runner beans, for instance, like their roots to be kept cool, and if fine compost or sedge peat is placed along the rows to a depth of an inch or so, and for 6 to 9 ins on either side of the rows, the 'mulching' is effective.

Other Operations The only other operations that might be mentioned are those of earthing-up and consolidation. For crops like onions it may be necessary to tread or roll the

soil before sowing seed or planting the onion sets. Light soils
are more often treated in this way than the clays. The
growth of crops like Brussels sprouts and onions is aided by
treading or rolling the soil before the crops are sown or
planted. After the rolling, the top inch or so needs lightly
cultivating to produce a surface tilth.

*Looking inside some
rhubarb forcing pots*

Some crops, like white celery, have to be earthed-up so as
to bleach them. Earthing-up prevents the green colouring
matter being produced in the stems, which may cause
bitterness. Some earthing-up not only bleaches but helps to
produce more tender, succulent celery. Seakale, chicory and
rhubarb are often forced or bleached by covering with pots
or whitewashed cloches, though seakale and chicory can be
produced by the ordinary earthing-up methods to the depth
of 10 ins or so.

Inorganic manures can never replace organic manures, and may in themselves be harmful. Humus is extremely important for vegetables. If the food value, flavour, and quality of vegetables are to be kept at a high level, the application of organic manures each year is essential.

Whether composted of animal manures or properly-made compost, humus assists in the aeration of soil and helps to produce a better mechanical and physical condition. Owing to the lack of humus and the constant application of artificial fertilizers, many of the earth's best soils have been turned into what may be described as 'desert lands'.

There are 250,000,000 acres in America which will never grow food again because of erosion – and also big acreages in India, South Africa, New Zealand, which also have been ruined by neglecting to add organic matter regularly.

Under poor soil conditions, insect pests and diseases are generally rife, and it is far more difficult to control them. If a plant is growing well, is healthy, and has sufficient space for development, it is robust enough to withstand attack, and therefore is seldom affected so badly. When good compost is used it will contain antibiotics which help to keep diseases at bay.

The author shows how every flower on the flowering stalk has set. There are no misses. This is what happens when you grow with compost only.

The main aim, then, of the vegetable gardener should be to try to supply sufficient organic matter which will provide humus. Once the organic material has been provided, organic fertilizers may play a useful part in stimulating crops and in supplying deficiencies. The aim of this book is to encourage everyone to produce vegetables of a high standard, full of vitamins, which can surely play an important part in preventing the diseases to which men are subject.

In olden days gardeners had little difficulty in obtaining large quantities of farmyard manure, but today well-made compost is used instead. Compost is not just a satisfactory substitute for farmyard manure – it is better than dung, vital to soil and therefore must be 'built up' each year.

Farmyard Manure Animal manures undoubtedly are valuable, not only for their content of organic material, but for the way in which they assist in liberating plant foods already present in soils. They differ greatly, however, in the amount of plant foods they contain.

Fresh manure, when dug in, has a harmful effect on soils

– scientists call it a de-nitrifying effect. Well-rotted old manure is valuable from the gardener's point of view, though difficult to obtain. When available, it is excellent as an activator in the compost heap, as a layer in between vegetable waste.

If farmyard manure alone is being used, it is difficult to give exact amounts, but, roughly speaking, apply one good barrow-load of well-rotted manure to 10 square yards.

The Compost Heap   Compost is no new method of feeding the soil. It has been practised for hundreds of years by the Chinese, who are experts at the intensive culture of vegetables. It is impossible to go into details of all the various processes, but one which has given excellent results and has been used at the Horticultural Training Centre run by the Good Gardeners' Association for a number of years is as follows :

A bin should be made of wood. It must be absolutely square, 4 ft x 4 ft – 6 ft x 6 ft – or 8 ft x 8 ft. One-in spaces may be left between the planks, to let in air. This bin is used to hold all the vegetable refuse from the house and garden : potato peelings, tea leaves, coffee grounds, dead flowers, rotting leaves, the tops of the peas and beans, hedge clippings – any plant matter that has lived.

These materials are put in to a depth of 6 in and are trodden level. A fish fertilizer is then sprinkled on at the

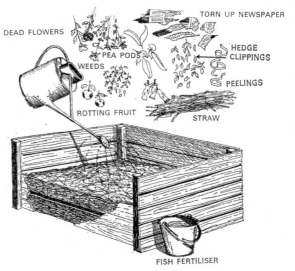

DEAD FLOWERS

TORN UP NEWSPAPER

PEA PODS

HEDGE CLIPPINGS

WEEDS

PEELINGS

ROTTING FRUIT

STRAW

FISH FERTILISER

rate of 3 oz per square yard. If the material is very dry a good watering is given. The quantity of water added depends on the dampness of the vegetable material used. It should never be sodden, just moist.

Successive 6-in layers are made as material becomes available. At the end of 6 months, or a somewhat longer period in the winter when the temperature is low, the compost is ripe. It is now a dark brown powder containing all the macro and micro nutrients. When the heap has risen to 6 ft the top is covered with a layer of soil 1 in deep.

Seaweed manure or dried poultry manure may be used instead of a fish manure. Brittle material, such as straw and the dead stems of herbaceous plants, should be sandwiched between layers of fresh green material, such as grass mowings and cabbage leaves. Where large quantities of fresh green materials are to be composted, they should either be allowed to wilt first, or sheets of newspaper may be put in between 2-in layers of lawn mowings or the like to prevent them becoming a sodden mass. Cabbage stumps should be beaten with the back of an axe on a chopping block before being used.

Sedge Peat This is forked into the top 2 ins at the rate of one bucketful to the square yard. Sedge peat may be used by beginners who have no home-made compost.

Dr Shewell-Cooper cuts away the side of a six-month-old compost heap. The bin is made with air spaces between the planks.

Green Manure One of the ways of adding organic matter to the soil is by means of 'green manure'. This consists of growing plants dug in shallowly long before they come to maturity. Unfortunately, green manures are slow in action, and it may take from the autumn to the spring before the green manures have fully rotted down.

The author levels off another layer of vegetable waste which he has just put on the compost heap. The heap is nearly complete.

Some 'green manures' like rye and mustard give back to the soil the food taken up during growth, but when members of the legume family are used – clovers, peas, vetches, lupins and so on – a good deal of nitrogen is collected from the air and is added to the soil. Some gardeners sow all the seeds they have over at the end of the season on a patch of land, and use those plants as 'green manure'.

Night Soil It is to be hoped that more and more town councils will compost dustbin wastes correctly with sewerage in order that they may be able to supply gardeners in their local areas with sufficient powdery compost in bags.

Meat and Bone Meal Meat and bone guanos are made from slaughter-house refuse – condemned meat and waste carcasses. This meal is usually applied at 4 to 5 oz per square yard a few weeks before sowing seed or planting out.

Hoof and Horn This is a slow-acting manure which contains nitrogen and phosphates but no potash. It is applied as for meat and bone meal.

Fish Manure This is a popular manure, and is offered

more or less free from objectionable odour. It is made from waste fish and fish residues. Without any additions it is rich in nitrogen and phosphates, but contains no potash. Some manufacturers add natural potash during drying and packing, and it then forms a complete manure. It is applied at 3 to 4 oz to the square yard, and gives good results. It is also used as the activator in compost heaps.

Spent Hops Spent hops are the residue left behind during the manufacture of beer. Hops contain no phosphates or potash and only a little nitrogen, but plants do root well in the organic medium they provide. They may be incorporated in the spring, or can be used as a top dressing along rows of plants during the summer.

The six-inch layers of vegetable waste in the compost heap are still visible at the end of the six-month period.

Seaweed Those who garden near the sea will find seaweed a practical substitute for organic manure. It is low in phosphates but is almost as valuable as the best old farm-yard manure, especially when properly rotted down. It can be applied as a top dressing in the autumn or may be used in the spring.

Soot Soot is a nitrogenous manure which can be used to lighten heavy soils. It darkens sandy soils and thus enables them to absorb and retain heat better. It is used, as a rule, as a top dressing in the spring. It is applied at 5 oz to the square yard.

Chemical Fertilizers Examined There are many gardeners who find that they can grow first-class crops without artificial fertilizers once they have 'built up' the humus content of their soils. I am one of them. Chemical fertilizers should certainly never be used alone. I would say never be used at all.

Fertilizers with an organic base, such as fish manure and poultry manure, do help the organic content of soil. These must not be classed as artificials.

The three plant foods normally deficient in any soil are nitrogen, phosphates and potash. Each has its own part to play in the building up of the vegetable, though some plants need more of one class of food than another. For instance, cabbages require more nitrogen, while peas need more phosphates.

It is useless to apply one of the substances in the hope that it will make up for a deficiency in another. These three plant foods must be present in the right proportions if perfect growth is to be obtained. The regular use of composted vegetable refuse (especially when the activator used is a seaweed or fish fertilizer) will ensure the provision of these three main plant foods – as well as supply all the trace elements, vitamins and antibiotics, making artificials unnecessary.

Nitrogen   Nitrogen helps to build up the stems and green leaves of the plant. Nitrogen-starved vegetables are light green in colour and generally small in size. The application of nitrogen will darken leaves and make them larger and more vigorous. Dried blood can be used for this purpose, at 1 oz to the yard run alongside crops.

Phosphates   The application of phosphates to the soil affects root growth. This increase in root production has, of course, an effect on the production of leaves later on. Phosphatic manures are especially needed by root crops.

Steamed Bone Flour   Steamed bone flour is a slow-acting manure. It is used for plants such as peas and beans that need a steady supply of phosphates throughout the season. It is used at 3 oz to the square yard and is organic.

Bone Meal   Bone meal contains gelatine, which the steamed bone flour does not. They are even slower in action and cannot be expected to give such good results. This is an organic fertilizer.

Rock Phosphates   Mineral phosphates are a natural form of phosphates and so can be recommended.

Potash   Where old farmyard manure is available, the application of potassic manures is not so important, for a ton of good, old, farmyard manure contains 15 lb of potash, equivalent to about 30 lb of sulphate of potash. Compost may easily contain a similar amount, or even more. Potash plays an important part in the production of firm, well-flavoured vegetables. It is needed by all crops, but particularly by peas and beans. It will help to produce pods of a better colour and of greater weight. Plants grown with sufficient potash have firm leaves which are resistant to disease. A healthier, better plant with strong fibre results from potash applications. The lighter soils are normally deficient in this plant food.

The chief potassic feeds that I use are wood ashes and flue dust. They are, of course, organic.

Wood Ashes These are only one-tenth as valuable as sulphate of potash, but are far quicker acting. Their value lies not only in the improvement of soil texture : they also provide a cheap form of plant food. They are useful too because they are organic in origin.

Flue Dust contains far less organic potash, but is often available when wood ashes are not.

Caution: Coal Ashes Mr J. Featherstone, – who has kindly checked through this chapter for me – examined many forms of coal ashes sent in by listeners as the result of my broadcast talks, and he found them to be definitely dangerous, chiefly because of the sulphur compounds they contain. I have known soils ruined by the use of coal ashes.

Liquid Manuring For generations gardeners have been using liquid manures, but no one was able to estimate correctly how such manures should be made up. The dilutions so often recommended used to make the solution the colour of weak tea. In the garden, liquid manure normally came from steeping animal droppings in water. Fortunately, certain firms now make up concentrated liquid manures which are sold in bottles to be diluted to a certain strength.

Liquid manure made from urine alone tends to be unbalanced and to produce coarse leafy plants. When it is made up with the more solid faeces, a complete liquid feed can be guaranteed. Urine, however, contains more trace minerals such as boron, iodine and magnesium than does solid excreta.

The bottled highly-concentrated liquid manures are quite clean and odourless after dilution. They are perfectly balanced and their standardized colour intensity is a safe guide to the method of dilution. Most are made from organic substances and from urea and so may be said to

contain dissolved humus. It is these dissolved organic substances in the bottled manures which undoubtedly act as a
stimulus to the bacteria.

For normal crops such as carrots, cabbage and onions,
use 4 gallons of the diluted manure per 30 ft row, when the
plants are about a quarter grown, and about 8 gallons per
30 ft row when the plants are half grown. With tomatoes,
I give a quart per plant immediately after the first truss has
set, half-a-gallon per plant after the second truss, and then
a gallon after the third and fourth trusses.

Lime   Lime is not only important in 'sweetening' soil and
preventing it from becoming acid, but is in itself a plant
food. The calcium in lime is valuable, and the basic part is
also valuable in neutralizing soil acids. On heavy soils, lime
improves the texture and the workability. Another function
of lime is to help release other plant foods : it helps to
decompose humus and organic compounds in the soil and
releases potash to be used as plant food.

Lime should always be used for the cabbage and the pea
and bean family, but it is not important for potatoes and
roots. Regular applications of lime usually make it possible
to keep down the club root disease. If applied at 7 oz to the
square yard once every three years, to the area where the
cabbage family is grown, it should keep the soil in good
condition.

Method of Application   Lime should never be dug in, for
it washes down into the soil very quickly. It should be
sprinkled on the surface of the ground, and will, of course,
be hoed in during the cultural operations. Lime should not
be mixed with farmyard manure.

Kinds of Lime   There are three main types of lime, the
most important of which to the vegetablue grower is

Hydrated Lime   This is convenient to handle, as it is generally sold in bags. It is not so valuable as quicklime.

Quicklime   Also sold as 'lump lime' or 'Buxton lime' (this
is sometimes ground into powder and sold as 'ground lime');
has to be slacked down on the soil. It is often difficult to
obtain.

Chalk or Limestone   Often sold as 'ground limestone', it
is half as valuable as quicklime, and must, therefore, be used
at a heavier rate. The usual rate of application is 7 oz to
the square yard of hydrated lime, and for ground lime 5 oz
to the square yard.

Though there is a law which prevents vegetable seeds of poor germination from being sold, no law stops a seeds merchant from selling a type which is not suited to certain conditions. For this reason the utmost care must be taken in selecting varieties that are of good flavour and crop heavily. There are far too many varieties on the market today, and many of them are synonymous. As far as possible, the name originally given to the variety is used in this book.

The greatest care should be taken in selecting a seeds merchant for the supply of vegetable seeds. It is advisable to obtain the seed from a firm that has been established for very many years and has a good reputation. Such firms usually have varieties of assured strains and high vitality.

Some seeds last longer than others, but to obtain the best results it is safer to buy new seed from your seeds merchant every year. Celery seed, for instance, may be kept for several years with success, but it is more economical to purchase the exact amount of seed that is required in a particular year than to buy larger quantities and hope to use the seed over a long period.

The Seedbed One of the first things the beginner has to learn is to prepare a seedbed. A properly prepared seedbed should contain the three essentials for successful germination, air, warmth and moisture. In order to produce these conditions a good deal of light forking and raking has to be done.

The bed, too, must be prepared in such a way that all the particles of soil are in a fine condition. After it has been completed, each particle of soil should be no larger than a grain of wheat. If the land is left rough, then the small seeds may fall into the crevices thus formed, or large portions of the unpulverized soil may bury them.

It is more difficult to get heavy soil into seedbed condition than light soil, and for this reason heavier clays should be prepared some time beforehand. Shallow cultivations and hoeings should be carried out regularly and systematically; it will be found that seeds will grow better than in soil which has been left undisturbed for some time.

Some seedbeds may be improved by the addition of lots of sand in the case of the heavy soils, and, in the case of the light soils, good powdery sedge peat. In heavy soils the sand helps aerate the soil, and in light soils it helps retain moisture and give a good medium into which the roots may grow.

Sowing the Seed Once the seedbed has been prepared the seed may be sown. Drills used should be of varying depths, depending on the size of the seed. A rough guide is that the seed should be sown to a depth three times its own width. Thus it will be seen that very small seeds have to be sown practically on the surface of the ground. Seeds also may be sown shallower in the spring, when the ground tends to be moist, than in midsummer, when the soil is usually dry.

There are two schools of thought with regard to seed-sowing : one believes in sowing thickly, because seed is cheap and it is always possible to thin out afterwards, and the other believes that thick seed sowing never gives the plants a chance in their earliest stages. This is probably the most important time in the life of the vegetable crop concerned. One would be wise to take the moderate course, sowing sufficiently thinly that seed is not wasted, and sufficiently early that the plants are not suffocated by one another.

It is possible to sow broadcast – that is, to distribute the seeds willy nilly over the surface of the ground – or to sow in straight, evenly spaced lines. The advantage of the latter method is that subsequent cultivations are far easier to carry out and all the plants get the same chance, the rows being at equal distances apart. The rows should first of all be marked out by means of a line and then the drills opened with a triangular hoe or the edge of a Dutch hoe. To obtain straight lines, be sure to keep the right foot on the line while working and the blade of the hoe up against the line when drawing the row.

Preparing a drill for sowing in the open.

Once the drills are opened out the seeds may be sown along them by hand. If the seed is taken in the palm and gently pushed out by means of the thumb and forefinger, an even distribution can be almost guaranteed. This method of sowing may need some practice before it becomes natural, but it is well worth the effort entailed. Until the beginner is perfect, the seeds may be placed in the palm of one hand and sprinkled carefully, as one would sprinkle salt, with the thumb and forefinger of the other.

With dark-coloured seeds it is advisable to mix them with a little hydrated lime first of all, so that the seeds may be seen easily when they reach the soil. In this way the evenness of the sowing can be more easily gauged.

There are today what are called 'pelleted seeds'. These are larger and much easier to sow thinly. Further, they are covered with plant foods and disease controllers.

Once in position, seeds may be covered up either by raking the soil over, using a rake in a backwards and forwards motion and in a straight line to prevent the seeds in the drill from being distributed outside them, or if the seeds are very small, they may be covered by sifting a little soil or sand over the rows.

On light land it is a good plan to tread the rows level or to beat them lightly with the back of the spade. This induces the moisture to rise to the surface and so help in the early germination of the seed. Once the little plants are through, hoeing should be done in between the rows, to prevent the rest of the moisture from evaporating into the atmosphere. If the rows are well marked by means of pegs, hoeing may be done before germination takes place.

TO ENSURE A STRAIGHT DRILL

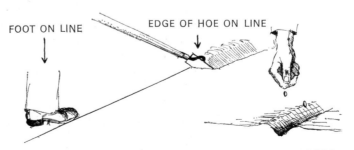

FOOT ON LINE

EDGE OF HOE ON LINE

HAVING MADE THE DRILL
SOW THE SEED THIS WAY

This allows moisture to rise to the actual place of germination and not up into space between the rows.

When sowings are made during the hot summer, a little shade may be given by a temporary structure of sacking or trellis. During very dry periods watering may be carried out, and during wet periods a certain amount of protection is often necessary.

Station Sowing A newish method of sowing known as 'station' sowing has much to recommend it. Instead of sprinkling the seeds along the drill, and then thinning the plants out later, three seeds are sown at 'stations' so many inches apart along the drill, the distance differing according to the type of vegetable. With beetroot that have to be thinned to 8 ins apart, three seeds should be sown at every 8 ins. With carrots that are normally thinned to 6 ins apart, three seeds are sown every 6 ins and so on. In order to provide an inter-crop of the same vegetable which may be pulled when half-grown, the usual plan is to sow at half stations, then thin down to one plant per station if each seed grows, and finally thin out every other plant when half grown, in order to leave the main 'plant' at the right distance. For example, if the beetroot are to be at 8 ins apart, station sowing would be done to 4 ins (i.e. three seeds at every 4 ins) and every other beetroot would be pulled out when the size of a golf ball so as to leave the remaining roots at the right distance, ie, 8 ins. These golf ball sized roots are delicious when cooked and prove a welcome change to mature beetroot.

The same rule can be applied to other crops.

Some seeds – particularly parsnips – are apt to germinate slowly, with the result that it is difficult to see exactly where the rows are. This difficulty is accentuated, naturally, in the case of long rows. For this reason it is customary to mix radish seed with the particular seed it is desired to sow. The radishes germinate quickly and show the actual line of the row, and in addition, prove a welcome catch-crop, as they are pulled and out of the way long before the main crop needs the room. This is a good method of ensuring thin sowing.

Thinning Thinning should be done as soon as it is possible to handle the seedlings. They should always be thinned with care and the best plants left in position; the weakest, and any which seem to show any peculiarities, should be removed. When thinning is done early in this way, the root systems have hardly had time to become established, and so the little plants come away easily and do not disturb their neighbours so much as if they were left in until a week or so later.

After thinning, the soil along the rows must be firmed and then well hoed. During very dry periods a good watering with a fine rose may also be necessary, and the hoeing, of course, should be done after this.

It is customary to thin the rows at two periods. In the first, the thinning is done to, say, half the distances ultimately intended for the crop, and in the second every other plant is removed. The advantage of this method is that in certain cases, like carrots and onions, fresh young plants are produced which do not interfere with the permanent crop, and so a type of catch-crop is made available. The pulling of the choice young roots naturally adds to the profit of the land concerned. This final thinning must never be delayed or the main crop will be harmed.

The seedlings produced in the seedbeds may be transplanted into other beds. This is often done in the case of lettuces, cabbages, endive, and the like, while even such root crops as beetroots and carrots may be transplanted in the earlier stages successfully.

Planting Out   Once good plants have been produced, it is a pity to ruin them by careless planting out. This does

Thinning out beetroot.

Planting onion sets.

not mean that the seedlings should be allowed to become too thick in the seedbed before they are moved. Plants raised in frames or glasshouses must never be put out into the open before they are sufficiently hardened off.

The land into which the plants are to be set should be prepared some time beforehand, and then, just before planting out, given a good raking or forking over. As in the case of seeds, the roots of the plants will appreciate soil that has been freshly stirred.

If transplanting can be carried out during a showery period, so much the better. If not, then a good watering may be given afterwards or the hole filled up with water as the plant is being put into position. Some people make up a mud puddle in a bucket and swish the roots of the plant round in this before they put them into the soil. On land that is subject to club root it may be necessary to put a solution of mercuric chloride into the hole before planting members of the 'cabbage' family.

To make certain that the plants will come out of the seedbed without injuring the roots, it is advisable to give the seedbed a thorough soaking of water the day before. In this way the plants themselves will be fresh and the leaves stiff, while the roots come away cleanly and do not break so easily. The plants will come out easily if the soil is forked well to loosen it between the little seedling rows. Once out of the ground, the plants should be put in water or kept in the shade until they can be put into their permanent position; the sooner they are planted there the better.

In the case of large plants, where obviously it is impossible to get them up without injuring the roots somewhat, shorten the leaves so as to balance up the root and leaf system. This is very useful in the case of cabbages and cauliflowers and is often done with onions and leeks as well.

Many people find a dibber satisfactory for making the hole for the seedling plant. Dibbers are good providing the plants are small and the root system has not developed considerably. With larger plants, a somewhat flattened trowel is advisable, as this can make a larger hole into which the roots may be spread.

When using a dibber, a hole should be made sufficiently large to take the plant, and the roots lowered into the hole, making quite certain that they are not turned upwards. The plant should go down so that the bottom seed-leaf rests on the surface of the soil, then the dibber is inserted diagonally at the side of the plant and the soil levered towards the bottom of the root. In this way the roots are planted firmly. There is no need to fill up this second hole made by the dibber, which provides a useful channel for watering.

Earlier Transplanting Beginners are often puzzled by the use of the term 'pricking out'. This means the transplanting of the little seedlings once, or perhaps twice, in their very early stages, generally under glass. Lettuces are often pricked out as soon as the seed leaves are large enough to handle. Very small holes have to be made with say a pencil, and it needs a good deal of practice to establish these tiny seedlings in their new position. Such pricking out ensures that practically every seedling raised comes to profitable maturity. Many market gardeners claim that early and frequent transplanting not only improves quality, but also hastens maturity.

Having prepared the box carefully, 'pricking out' takes place putting in the seedlings with a dibber about 2 inches apart.

5 Crop Rotations

As an adviser in various parts of the country I have found again and again that crops are ruined by certain diseases, largely because rotational principles are neglected.

Rotation is a system by which vegetables of the same character do not follow one another on the same piece of ground year after year. The use of the words 'vegetables of the same character' is important, and allows for crops not necessarily related to be grown side by side for some reason other than their affinity. For instance, one can classify the deep-rooting crops together, or the shallow-rooting crops. Vegetables like peas and beans, that enrich the soil with nitrogen, can all go into one group. Each may require certain manures and treatment. Thus by keeping vegetables of the same character together it is possible to deal with them largely as one.

This is the first step towards rotation, i.e. seeing that each group is grown in one particular part. The next step is to see that the group does not remain on the same plot of land year after year. Take the pea and bean family, for instance : they have the power to add nitrogen to the soil; they do not necessarily need this nitrogen themselves; sensible gardeners therefore grow peas and beans in different parts of the garden every year, so that each part in its turn may be enriched at no cost to themselves.

Land which receives the same treatment year after year tends to deteriorate. Rotation prevents the exhaustion of a particular plant food in the soil. A particular crop may take from the soil large quantities of certain plant foods, and so the growing of this crop, or group of crops, on one plot of land may tend to impoverish the soil in some respects.

One crop can leave the land in better condition for another. The peas and beans leave nitrogen of which the cabbage family can make much use, and so better cabbage crops result.

It is possible, by means of rotations, to keep down pests and diseases. The obvious example is Club Root. When members of the cabbage family are grown for years on the same piece of land, the club root disease tends to increase year after year, until, as is the case with many allotments in England, cabbages are practically impossible to grow. If rotations had been carried out, the cabbage crop would never have been on one plot of land more than one year in four, and this would have given a chance of eradicating the disease. Pests too, like carrot fly, find it far easier to damage a crop if the carrot seeds are sown directly on top of the place where the chrysalids lie buried after the previous year's attack.

Some plants excrete toxins or 'poisons'. These toxins accumulate after a time, when plants are grown on the same land continuously, and are harmful. They are, curiously enough, harmless to other crops. Land that is known to be 'cauliflower sick' will grow good crops of peas and beans. Soil sickness is not easily explainable, but it is advisable not to take a chance of toxins developing.

To sum up, it can be said that rotations are an economy of labour. They make for the keeping down of weeds and they allow for periods when green manuring may be carried out. Any rotational scheme gives an opportunity for liming. The break on which cabbages are to be grown will be limed

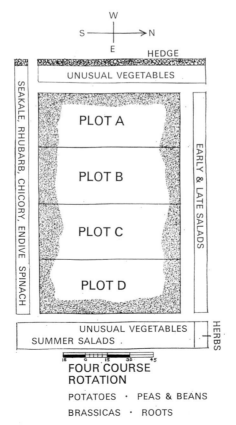

FOUR COURSE
ROTATION

POTATOES · PEAS & BEANS
BRASSICAS · ROOTS

fairly heavily, while peas and beans will have just a light dressing. Most people welcome any scheme that will help them to be methodical, and if rotations do nothing else, they do help in this way.

When planning rotations, remember :

1 That peas and beans leave the land rich in nitrogen, especially if the roots are left in.

2 That root crops, such as carrots and beetroot, will fork if given plenty of fresh manure, and so they are better grown on land that was well manured the year before.

3 That more permanent crops, which may interfere with rotation, should be grown on a plot of their own.

4 That dwarf crops and tall ones should if possible, be interspersed to allow light and air to reach all the crops.

THREE-COURSE ROTATION This is the simplest rotation of all. For this the garden is divided into three parts, and the

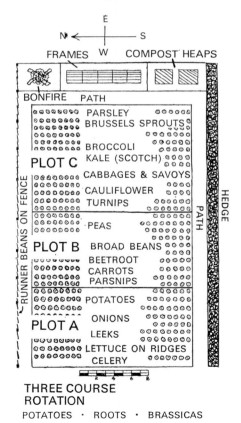

THREE COURSE
ROTATION
POTATOES · ROOTS · BRASSICAS

vegetables that are to be grown have to be classified into three groups also. The three-course rotation is by no means perfect, but it does ensure that some methodical moving round of crops takes place. The three large groups usually adopted for this purpose are:

1 The cabbage family, which will include the Brussels sprouts, cauliflowers, etc.
2 The root crops.
3 The group consisting mainly of potatoes.

It is very difficult to get three large groups, but it will be seen that deep-rooting crops do alternate with the shallow-rooting ones. For fear of club root, turnips should be classified with the cabbage family.

FOUR-COURSE ROTATION This is the rotation usually adopted, and it is comparatively easy to divide all the crops up into four large groups:

Group 1 Early potatoes, second early potatoes, and perhaps, if necessary, the main crop, though these are often grown on their own.

Group 2 The pea and bean family: runner beans, broad beans, French beans, and peas; and here, if necessary, the celery, leeks, onions, and shallots may be included. (Those who need few potatoes should grow celery, leeks and onions on the potato break.)

Group 3 The root crops: parsnips, carrots, beetroot, salsify and scorzonera.

Group 4 The Brassica family, ie, cabbages, cauliflowers, Brussels sprouts, kale, kohlrabi, turnips and swedes.

Notice that certain other crops have not been included – lettuce and spinach, for instance – but these may be grown as intercrops or catch-crops wherever possible, without interfering with the main scheme. Chives and parsley can make edgings, and the permanent crops can be planted, together on their own. The plans on pp. 35-6 should explain how the rotations are worked. It will be seen that in the case of the three-course rotation the main scheme is potatoes, then roots, then Brassicas; while in the four-course the idea is that potatoes should be followed by peas, then by Brassicas; and finally by the roots. Alternative plans are possible, so that it will be seen that there are no hard and fast rules in this connection.

Artichoke
Globe

This large thistle-like plant is grown for the sake of its large flower heads. The leaf scales of these are used as the vegetable.

Soil This crop does best in a deep, rich, moist soil, and better heads are produced if the plants are grown in a sunny situation. Should the land be heavy, it may be improved by the use of compost or sedge peat. Artichokes may die out on wet soils during severe weather if they are not protected or if the soil is not lightened in some way. It is in the summer that the artichokes need moisture, not in the winter.

Manuring Before planting, compost should be applied to the ground at the rate of one good barrow-load per 12 square yards. In addition, use fish fertilizer at 3 oz to the square yard. In the spring, when the plants are growing, dried blood may be used at 1 oz to the yard run. Every year, during the spring, a liberal dressing of compost and a similar quantity of fish manure may be applied between the rows.

Propagation It is possible to raise plants from seed, though one cannot rely on the best varieties coming true to type. If seed has to be sown, sow it thinly in a box containing NO-SOIL Compost, in a greenhouse, at a temperature of 55°F in February. Directly the seedlings are large enough to handle, pot them up into 3-in pots and grow them on in a cold frame. They may then be hardened off gradually until they are planted out into their permanent positions in the second week in April.

It is better to propagate by means of suckers, which should be cut from the old plants with a sharp knife when they are about 9 ins high. Each sucker should have a portion of root attached to it. It is advisable to do this during November, and then to pot up each sucker, standing the pots in a cold frame for the winter. The plants are then ready to be put out at the same time as the seedlings.

It is also possible to remove the suckers in April and plant them out immediately in rows 4 ft apart, the plants themselves being 3 ft apart in the rows. The suckers are put in 4 ins deep and the land then trodden firmly and watered well. During a hot spring it may be necessary to give a certain amount of shade until the plants are well established.

Slugs often attack globe artichokes, and to prevent this a little circle of coarse sedge peat is sometimes put around each plant. In May, should the weather be dry, a mulching with straw may be given, with occasional waterings. Flowers should never be allowed to develop the first year.

GENERAL CULTIVATION Regular weeding should be carried out, unless the whole area has been mulched with powdery compost or sedge peat, in which case annual weeds will not grow. The plants may also be disbudded, i.e. the lateral heads or buds removed when they are about the size of an egg. The advantage of leaving the laterals until this stage is that they can be fried or eaten raw.

In the autumn, after all the heads have been cut, the stems may be cut down, together with the large leaves. The smaller central leaves should not be touched, as these will protect the crown.

In districts where severe frosts can be expected, draw the soil up to the little plants and throw a little dry straw over them. In the spring remove this litter and draw back the earth level again. Never leave a "plantation" of artichokes down longer than five years.

Harvesting Before the petals appear cut off the flowering heads while they are still young and tender and just before they are fully developed. If they are left on the plant too long they become coarse. They are usually cut with a stem 6 ins long, and this is then stood in water under cover until required. The main heads are always the best. If the laterals are not removed in the early stages they produce a second crop.

Varieties One of the best varieties is *Grand Camus de Bretagne*, though the large *Green Globe* is much liked because it is devoid of prickles.

Artichoke Jerusalem

This vegetable is a hardy herbaceous perennial, and I leave the row down for 12 years and more. However, most gardeners replant it every year.

Soil The Jerusalem artichoke will grow in almost any soil and will produce heavy crops despite very indifferent treatment. Grow in an open situation and manure like potatoes.

Manuring In addition to the organic manure used, apply 3 oz of fish fertilizer per sq. yard a fortnight before planting.

Propagation The propagation is done by means of tubers saved from the previous year's crop. The tubers should be about the size of a pullet's egg. If the tubers are larger they may be cut, providing there are three eyes to each.

Planting Rows should be made 2½ ft apart and the tubers planted 12 ins apart in the rows and 6 ins deep.

PLANT JERUSALEM ARTICHOKES

General Cultivation Directly the plants are through the ground, mulch the rows with compost or sedge peat. Towards the end of November cut the stems down to within 1 ft of the ground.

Harvesting Lift the whole crop up at one time and store the tubers in sand, or lift a few roots as they are required. When lifting, take care not to damage the artichokes. Any medium-sized tubers may be selected for planting for the following season. The largest tubers may be stored in sand or put into a clamp.

Varieties *New White* has a more delicate flavour than the old-fashioned purple variety. *Fuzeau* is a variety which has smooth tubers with no knobs on them – my favourite kind.

Asparagus

For some strange reason asparagus is looked on as a luxury, and this makes the ordinary man frightened of growing it. Yet an asparagus bed is comparatively easy to lay down and costs little to maintain, so there is no reason at all why all gardens should not have a row or two.

Soil It is possible to grow this crop successfully in almost any soil if good drainage is provided.

Manuring There is need for generous manuring. Apply good compost every autumn, after the asparagus foliage has been cut down. In addition, organic fertilizers may be used – say 4 oz of a good fish fertilizer per square yard. Dried blood may be given in the spring at the rate of 2 oz to the square yard, directly growth becomes active.

Propagation It is possible to raise plants by sowing seed, but this operation is generally left to the nurseryman. Those who wish to obtain quick returns should purchase three-year-old plants. It is generally better to plant one-year-old plants, though this means waiting two or more years before a crop can be cut.

Planting Plant up single rows 4 ft apart, with the plants 2 ft apart in the rows. Some prefer rows 3 ft apart, with the plants 18 ins in the rows, while others like double rows 4 ft apart with 18 ins between the rows and 18 ins between the plants.

If one-year-old plants are used, they should have three or four good strong buds at the crown. Two or three-year-old plants will naturally look stronger. It should be possible to put the plants into position early in April, and if planting can be done on a mild day, so much the better. Take out a

trench 8 ins wide and 8 ins deep and spread out the spidery-looking roots of the asparagus evenly in this trench. If the plant is set upon a little mound of soil, it will be easier to put the roots naturally into position. (They are rather like the legs of a huge spider!) It also will ensure that the crown (or the growing bud part) of the plant is about 4 ins below the soil level after covering in.

The young plant's roots should never be exposed to dry winds or the sun, and it should be planted promptly. If this is impossible cover the plants with a damp sack and keep out of the sun's rays. It is advisable to make the beds ready, so that when the parcel is delivered the plants can be unpacked and put in immediately.

Two people can plant asparagus more quickly than one – one person holding the plant in position and spreading out the roots and the other putting over the soil so that this can be trodden down carefully. In order to assist recognition of the rows during the early stages it is a good idea to put a strong stake at either end.

General Cultivation During the first year or two, small crops are often grown between the rows. Radishes, lettuces, and spring onions are suitable catch-crops.

Watch the beds and if you find blank spaces towards the middle of June, obtain further plants and plant them immediately, making certain to water them in. Throughout the season hoe lightly on either side of the rows or beds – unless a complete mulching with sedge peat has been carried out, in which case hoeing is unnecessary.

In the late autumn cut down the foliage close to the ground. Never allow the female plants to let their berries ripen and drop on to the soil – unprofitable seedlings will appear.

Owing to the fragile stems they may snap off at the base. It is usual in windy situations to give the feathery growth some support when well grown. A bamboo or two at the ends of the rows and green twine run in between them forms an effective support.

There is a slight difference of opinion among experts as to whether the rows should be earthed-up in the winter or the spring. Some prefer February, others late March. As the crowns grow larger they naturally need more soil and compost to cover them, and so the ridges tend to become higher. Owing to the growth of the plants during the summer the soil may fall away, so that by the time the foliage is cut down again the ridges have practically disappeared.

Experiments have shown that male asparagus plants (the plants which bear no berries) give a 60-90 per cent higher yield than the female plants, so obviously you should try to remove the females and concentrate on the males only!

Harvesting Do not cut until the third year. Every year, however, cutting should cease by the end of June, and, during the first two cutting years, about the beginning of June. During the harvesting time the thinner shoots should be left to grow, *ie*, only the thicker ones should be cut. When cutting ceases, all the shoots are left.

Cut with a long, strong, narrow-pointed knife. This is plunged into the ridge, severing the stick just above the crown without injuring the latter. Take care not to injure other younger sticks that are coming through at the same time. Cut when the brownish-green tips of the shoots are 3 or 4 ins above soil level.

Varieties *Early Argenteuil* is said to be the earliest, and under good conditions it may be cut from the beginning of April onwards. *Connover's Colossal*, originally an American variety is later, and has slender pointed buds. *K.B.*, an English 'strain' which has given excellent results, produces large delicious 'buds' in abundance and is probably the best asparagus today.

Bean, Broad

Soil The broad bean is not particular as to soil, and will grow as readily on heavy land as on the lighter ones.

Preparation of Soil No special preparation is needed. In the case of autumn sowings which follow previously sown crops, only a light raking is necessary.

Manuring The autumn-sown beans require no special manuring, but those sown in the spring may have a light dressing of compost lightly raked in 3 weeks before sowing the seed. In addition, 3 oz of fish manure should be added. Sedge peat can be applied at one bucketful to the square yard.

Sowing the Seed Sow seeds outside either in November or from early to mid-March. Where frames or cloches are available, sowing is done in December or January, and the young plants raised in frames put out into the permanent position during the second or third week of March.

It is always necessary to plant on a dry day. When soil

conditions are unfavourable it is better to delay sowing for a few days.

The *Longpod* types are usually sown in November and January and the *Windsors* in March. November sowings may not come through owing to frost or wet weather.

The rows should be 2½ ft apart, the drills 5–6 ins wide, and a double row of beans put into these drills staggered so that they are 6 ins apart. The drills would be prepared 2 ins deep. The double row is generally successful because it allows of a heavier yield per plot of land without impairing the efficiency of the plants.

It is advisable to sow 12 beans in a group at the ends of the rows, as these may be planted out later on when 3 or 4 ins high, if any gaps appear.

General Cultivation The soil should be kept clean between the rows. Keep a sharp look-out for the black aphis, and, directly it appears, apply a derris dust or spray. It is not necessary to pinch out the tops except to encourage the early production of beans. Directly the crop is over, cut down the tops and leave the roots in the ground. The tops should be put on the compost heap.

Harvesting Pick the beans regularly, as this ensures a heavier crop. Pick on the young side.

Varieties Longpods: *Longfellow,* a very early tall-growing variety bearing enormous pods. *Gillett's Imperial Longpod,* bears large, well-filled pods of good flavour. *Windsors:* Grow a good seedsmen's strain, i.e. *Gillett's Imperial Windsor.* Smallpods: *Dwarf Bush,* grows 1 ft high and is quick maturing. If sown as late as July will give a crop the same year.

Bean, French, Dwarf or Kidney

The French bean comes into cropping earlier, and is sown earlier than its cousin the runner bean. It can be sown in pots under glass, in pots under frames, in the south border to secure a crop early in the season, and in the main garden as late on as June in order to get a picking towards the end of September.

Soil Being a 'legume', it will enrich the soil. It withstands drought better than any other vegetable crop.

Preparation of Soil Fork the soil lightly, adding powdery compost at the same time as two bucketfuls to the square yard. In the spring the land where the French beans are to be grown may be cropped with lettuce, and these will give

some protection to the young plants as they come through. The lettuce should be cut as the French beans grow.

Manuring Apply fish manure at 3 oz per square yard and wood ashes at 4 oz per square yard. Should the plants be affected by a bad spell of weather after they come through, apply dried blood along the rows at 1 oz to the yard run and water. Lime is generally necessary for members of the pea and bean family, and may be applied to the surface of the ground after the raking in of fish manure at from 4 to 7 ozs per square yard, depending on the acidity of the soil.

Sowing the Seed The first sowing outside is done during the first week of May, or even earlier in the south-west. In this case the 'nurse' crop will already be growing well, and drills should be made 2 ins deep, and from 2 to 3 ft apart, depending on the variety. In each drill the seeds are 4 ins apart. Some gardeners prefer to sow twice as thickly as this, and then to thin out and transplant either into the gaps or into further rows. If this is not done, plant a few extra seeds at the end of one of the rows – to provide spares.

The last sowing is done the first week in July without the 'nurse' crop, with the rows 2 ft apart and the beans spaced 8 ins apart. The soil for these later sowings never need be specially prepared. It can be covered with cloches in mid or late September.

General Cultivation Hoe between the rows and draw the soil up to the plants rather than away from them. Clear the 'nurse' crop as soon as the plants are growing well.

In the case of tall varieties, the plants may need supporting with bushy twigs, if the situation is too exposed.

Harvesting Pick French beans when they are young. Regular gathering will prevent the swelling of seeds in the pods.

Varieties Dwarfs: *The Prince* is undoubtedly the best early French bean today. Crops very heavily. *Masterpiece,* an excellent variety which bears long handsome pods and crops heavily. *Processor,* the variety insisted on by the canners. It is stringless and of superb flavour and quality. *Pencil Pod Black Wax,* sometimes known as the Waxpod bean and sometimes the Golden Butter bean. This variety bears very delicious golden French beans.

The Blue Runner bean called 'Blue Coco' is delicious and crops heavily.

Bean Runner

Soil Runner beans grow well in practically all soils.

Preparation of Soil Where the runner beans are to be

grown, the ground should be liberally mulched with powdery compost or sedge peat in late March or in early April. Lightly fork this in.

Manuring It is difficult to say how much compost is really necessary, as heavy amounts have to be used. One large barrowload, for instance, may only do 6 ft or so. Fish manure should be added at 3 oz per square yard and should be raked in. Hydrated lime should be applied to the surface of the ground at the rate of 3 ozs to the square yard, if the soil is known to be acid.

Sowing Runner beans cannot be sown early because they will not germinate unless the soil is warm. Sowing is generally possible by the second week of May. Another sowing may be made towards the beginning of June.

The rows, when they are to grow up poles, should be 5 ft apart, and the seeds sown 2 ins deep and 9 ins apart. Where runner beans are to be grown on the flat, the rows may be 4 ft apart, the seeds being sown at 4 ins apart in the rows.

Thinning If the beans are sown thickly, thinning has to be carried out when the beans are 2 ins high. Space out 9 ins apart.

Transplanting If a number of beans are sown in a group at the end of the rows, then these may be transplanted

Sowing runner beans in staggered fashion.

Runner beans grown with compost only in the author's garden. The crops are extraordinarily heavy.

when they are 3 ins high into any blank spaces that may appear in the rows.

It is possible also to sow the seeds in boxes under glass, to obtain earlier crops. Such sowing may be done in boxes at least 4½ ins deep at the end of April, and the plants thus raised in the greenhouse planted out early in June.

Staking Put the poles in position just after sowing, or just before, 9 ins apart. These poles generally cross at the top for the end, say 6 ins, and poles may be laid across the V's thus made. If the cross poles and the poles laid on lengthways are then lashed together, a very firm structure is made.

If it is impossible to obtain a large number of stakes, strands of string may be used stretched from wire running along the ground and at the tops of the few poles available. Wire netting has the advantage of being usable for several years.

Those with very small gardens will find it convenient to have a little group of strong poles or bamboos going up like an Indian Tepee. Have this near a path or at the corner of a border. The runner beans can clamber up these 'tepees' and the effect is not only beautiful but practical.

General Cultivation Light hoeing should be carried out, not only along the rows but in between the plants also. All hoeing should be up to the rows rather than away from them. Early in July a mulch of sedge peat may be put along the rows to keep the moisture in the soil. This should be done after a heavy watering, in a dry season. Regular waterings in a dry year will not only make for better pods, but will prolong the cropping period. In the evening the rows may be sprayed with water to help the flowers to set and to keep the pods tender.

Harvesting The beans should be picked regularly. Pods that have to be picked in order to prevent them from seeding may be kept fresh for several days if their stem ends are put in a saucer of water.

Varieties *Hammond's Dwarf Scarlet* is an early dwarf variety which crops 14 days earlier than any other type. The best kind for growing 'on the flat'. *Hammond's Dwarf White* is similar to Dwarf Scarlet. *Streamline* is a valuable exhibition variety, the favourite mainly because it is so tender. *Crusader*, a very large podded variety, is never coarse. Beans hang in large clusters – they are large but tender.

Beetroot

Beetroot is generally grown too large, consequently it tends to be coarse. It is usually considered only suitable to accompany cold meat as a kind of pickle or in salads. Recently, however, it has become quite a fashionable vegetable when cooked and served hot, either mashed with butter, or whole. It may also be served as fritters.

Soil   Probably the best soil for beetroot is a light loam which has a good depth. However, properly conditioned clays can also be suitable.

Preparation of Soil   It is not necessary to dig in large quantities of farmyard manure or coarse compost for beetroot; this tends to cause the beetroot to fork. If the crop can follow one that has been well manured previously, all is well.

Shallow forking is advised in the early spring. Let some time elapse between that and the making of the seedbed, to allow the soil to settle. Long beetroot grows well on land that has carried celery or leeks the previous year. Early in May the soil where the beetroot is to be sown may be forked over and then raked down finely.

Manuring   Though it is not necessary to add compost to the land, seaweed may be used with advantage. Apply a barrowload to 10 square yards, and fork in lightly. A good fish manure can be applied at the rate of 4 oz to the square yard ten days before sowing the seed, and should be lightly forked in.

Sowing the Seed   Sow the seed either at the end of April or at the beginning of May, in rows 15 ins apart, the little drills being 1 in deep. On heavy clays, especially in the bleaker parts of the north, it may not be possible to sow until after the middle of May.

Seeds may be sown thinly in the drills, but regular sowing is necessary. After sowing, cover the drills and make sure the surface of the bed is left level.

Some of the smaller globe varieties grown as early crops may be sown in rows as close as 1 ft apart. Make these earlier sowings in a sunny south border at any time from the end of March to the middle of April, depending on the weather and the district. Protect the earlier sowings with fish netting, as birds are most partial to the seedlings. A late spring frost will also damage them. In this instance the seeds are sown only 1½ ins deep.

Further sowings of the early globe varieties may be made

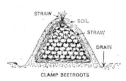

CLAMP BEETROOTS

in July, so as to obtain delicious little roots in the autumn and winter. Sowing is done as advised in the previous paragraph. Broadcast sowings are also possible, providing these are done thinly.

Thinning   Thin the rows so that the plants are 8 ins apart. This is done at two periods, in the first place when the plants are 3 ins high to half the distance, and then, when they are the size of golf balls, to the full distance. In this way the later thinnings may be used in the house. For the early crops in the south border it is only necessary to thin to 6 ins in the rows, and this holds good for the late July sowings also.

Transplanting   It is possible to transplant the young beetroot seedlings if necessary. Sometimes gaps occur in rows for no apparent reason, and these may be filled in at the first thinning. When transplanting is carried out, a good watering should be given every day during dry weather until the plants are well established.

Clamping beetroot.

General Cultivation Regular hoeing is as necessary for beetroot as any other crop, but these have to be done more carefully. Never damage the roots with the hoe, for if they bleed the colour is lost. There is no need to bring the soil up to the rows.

Apart from the watering of the thinnings, it is usually a waste of time to water the crops. Beetroot is fairly easy to grow providing the initial cultivation is well done.

Harvesting Beetroot may be left in the ground until it is needed in the winter, providing it is covered with straw, bracken or cloches during severe frosts. It is generally safer to lift the roots and to store them in a clamp, as for potatoes. Cut off the tops before storing, but never too near to the crown or bleeding may take place. Beetroot may be stored in sand or dry earth in a shed, and if this has to be done it should be dug up before the middle of October. If well stored, it will keep until the following June.

The long types of beetroot may have the end of the tapering root removed without much harm being done. Apart from this, beetroot should always be handled carefully as they suffer from rough treatment.

Varieties *Asmer Empire Globe* : a variety which bears beautiful globe-shaped beets which when cut through will be found to be of a dark crimson colour and free from white rings. *Detroit Selected Globe* : The canner's favourite. A very dark red strain, with small roots. *Crimson Globe Improved* : Said to be the earliest strain of all. Has very few leaves. *Spangsbjerg Cylinder* : The best known Intermediate. Delicious, a longish, oval shape. *Show Bench* : The most popular exhibition variety, giving roots of excellent colour. *Boltardy* : Retains its colour, even when cut into slices before cooking. Does not go to seed like other kinds. *Burpee's Golden* : A golden orange globe beet. Does not bleed. The leaves can be boiled and served as spinach.

Broccoli

There are three types of broccoli, the first producing a beautiful white head similar to that of the cauliflower, and sometimes called the winter cauliflower, the second producing a large number of purple sprouts, and the third yielding a profusion of agreeably flavoured white 'sprouts'. The cultivation of the two latter types are described under the heading of 'Broccoli, Sprouting.'

So intermingled have the cauliflower and broccoli become

that it is almost impossible today for an expert to say where the cauliflower ends and the broccoli begins.

Soil Broccoli will grow in most soils, but it prefers a clay or a heavy loam. Light sandy soils must be made firm, or open curds result.

Preparation of Soil Broccoli prefers firm soil, and so the wise gardener plants his crop on land that has been well prepared for a previous crop. There is no need to do any special preparation in consequence.

Manuring Mulch the light lands 1 in deep with a large barrowload of compost to 8 square yards. Fork this in and firm. Fish manure may be applied at 3 oz to the square yard, just before planting.

Sowing the Seed Sow the seeds of most varieties of broccoli during the second week in April. The sowing of the June varieties may be delayed until the middle of May. The seed is sown in drills from half-inch deep.

After sowing, some protection from birds is needed. Black cotton strung from short pieces of bamboo is usually effective.

The rows in the seedbed should be 6 ins apart. Rake the soil down finely before sowing. Once the seeds are through hoe the rows to keep down weeds. Before the seedlings get too long and lanky thin and transplant them into further seedbeds, 6 ins between the rows and 3 ins apart. This pricking out of the seedlings ensures first-class plants, and consequently better heads in the autumn.

Planting Broccoli is a useful crop to follow crops that have been harvested early. Broccoli grows well after early potatoes, French beans, or even peas.

As soon as the land is ready, put out the plants to prevent them from becoming lanky in their seedbed. Plant in rows 2½ ft apart, the plants 2 ft apart. In the case of the small varieties, the rows may be 2 ft and the plants only 18 ins apart. The advantage of close planting is that the plants give some protection to each other. Firm the ground when planting, as loose soil produces loose curds. Gapping up may be done a fortnight after planting out.

General Cultivation In milder districts nothing need be done. In cases where the soil is wet and the winter hard the plants may be pushed over so that the heads incline to the north, by taking away a little soil from that side and, after pushing the plants over, placing the soil on the other

side of the plants. If this work is done during November, the plants will be helped over the future frosty periods.

Apart from this, hoeing should be done until the weeds cease to grow.

Harvesting Cut the curds directly they are ready, and if too many 'turn in' at a time, break off a leaf or two and put over the white head.

Varieties Autumn: *Veitch's Self-Protecting.* This produces pure white, close heads, which are generally well protected. *Early Cornish* or *Penzance.* Turns in in November and December, specially suited for the south and south-west.

Winter or Early Spring: *Veitch's Self-Protecting Autumn.* A favourite variety in the southern districts, good where there are no severe frosts. Sow seed in March. *Leamington.* First-class, used during March and April. *Snow's Superb Winter White.* A robust and hardy variety which matures in December, throwing large heads. *Roscoff.* Cut in February and March.

Spring: *Markanta.* Cut in April or May in the south-west and some time later in other areas. Produces beautiful pure white heads. *Armado April.* A new type of broccoli which stands well under northern conditions. It produces medium-sized heads, pure white in colour.

Late Spring or Early Summer. *Cluseed Royal Oak.* Another hardy variety suited for the midlands and north, it comes into cutting in May. *Cluseed May Blossom.* Turns in in mid-May. Good southern variety. *Late Queen.* A dwarf and compact grower, rarely affected by frosts; may be cut May and early June. One of the really well-protected types. *Asmer Midsummer.* A very hardy variety, suitable to be grown under northern conditions, it is somewhat of a dwarf grower, but throws a good curd. *Whitsuntide.* A late variety for the south, which throws a large pure white curd at Whitsuntide.

Unwin's Calabrese a delicious type of sprouting broccoli.

Broccoli, Sprouting

No garden should be without this excellent winter crop. The sprouting broccoli throws a large number of small white flower-heads which are delicious. The sprouting broccoli is hardier than ordinary broccoli.

The seeds may be sown in April and the plants put out 2 ft square. Treat them well and they will produce an abundant crop. The purple variety is preferred to the white type. The late purple is the hardiest.

Harvesting   Do not cut sprouting broccoli until the flower-shoots are growing out from in between the axils of the leaves. Cut these down to within two-thirds of their length, and as a result more shoots are thrown out on the same little stem. At the end of the season practically the whole plant will have to be consumed.

Varieties *Calabrese Green Comet*: This very early sprouting broccoli which has a particularly good flavour, is used in September. The shoots should be gathered immediately, as they quickly run to seed. Sow in March. *Calabrese Late Corona*: Similar to Green Comet but much later. *Early Purple Sprouting*: A very compact grower, and one which will often be fit to cut from December–February. Cut shoots when 9–12 ins long. *Late Purple Sprouting*: Will withstand the most severe frosts and yet will grow away quickly as soon as the weather becomes milder; it comes into cutting in April and gives a beautiful green colour. *White Sprouting*: Comes in at the same time as Early Purple – but it is not so hardy.

Brussels Sprouts

The Brussels sprout is one of the crops that must be well grown to be profitable. There are four points that should be borne in mind when attempting to cultivate this crop.

1 Sow early because they need a long season of growth.
2 Provide plenty of room for development.
3 Manure heavily.
4 Firm ground preferred.

SOIL   This crop is not particular as to soil.

Preparation of Soil   The ground should always be firm so that the sprouts will form really large, firm, 'buttons'. Firmness of soil cannot be over-emphasized. I have seen successful gardeners put sprout plants out into land in which it was very difficult even to make the holes for planting! There is little need to do special deep cultivation.

Manuring   A well-piled-up barrowload of properly prepared compost should be used to 8 square yards. Fish manure should be used at 3 ozs to the square yard. If the sprouts are not growing satisfactorily, soot may be applied at 4 ozs per yard run as a tonic in early September.

Seed Sowing   Make the first sowing at the end of February or early in March, in a frame. Sow the seeds in

This is the Sanda Brussels sprout, a very heavy cropper

rows 3 ins apart and the plants thinned out to 2 ins apart when they are fit to handle. Make the next thin sowing in early April and transplant the seedlings into their permanent positions directly they are fit to handle. Whenever plants are raised in a seedbed pick out the largest plants at the first transplanting, and then to go over the original bed a fortnight later and pick out the next largest, and to do this three or four times. In this way, successive batches of plants of different sizes can be obtained from one sowing.

Planting The plants should be put out during May, or perhaps early June, in rows 2½ ft apart, the plants being at least 2 ft apart in the rows. For the tall, heavy cropping varieties the plants need 3 ft square. If the planting can be done during a showery period, so much the better, but, if not, the plants must be watered in.

It should be possible to sow intercrops between the rows, and spinach, radish, or lettuce are quite suitable for this purpose. Occasionally hoe lightly in the summer to kill weeds, but take care during hoeing to avoid injuring the leaves. Never remove the leaves of the sprout plants until they are turning yellow and decaying. The head of the plant should not be removed until the end of February.

Harvesting When the sprouts are picked it is advisable to cut them off, leaving a short stalk on the main stem, rather than to break them off. These little short sprout stems will then throw further loose open sprouts. Pick systematically, starting from the bottom of the stem and working up. All the plants should be gone over. It is wrong to pick sprouts from one or just a few plants, leaving the others untouched.

Varieties *Continuity.* An extra early variety which produces large solid sprouts that cover stems of medium height. *Sanda.* Produces fine solid sprouts on a strong growing stem. A splendid variety for the deep freeze. *Cambridge Late No. 5.* A handsome tall-grower which produces fine sprouts from the ground upwards. Can be picked fairly early when of moderate size, but retains large sprouts until late in the season. *Irish Elegance* : A mid-season strain which is excellent in the midlands. A high quality sprout. *Cluseed Giant.* A tall variety – first-class for the north. *Clucas Favourite.* Another tall northern variety studded with solid sprouts. An abundant cropper. *Prince Askold.* A semi-tall strain, much liked in Bedfordshire and adjoining counties. A late solid sprout. *King of the Lates.* The latest variety of all. Usually picked three weeks after any other kind. Medium to tall stem.

Cabbage

There are a large number of types of cabbage. The main ones are the spring, summer and winter varieties. It is possible to keep up a supply of cabbages all the year round. SOIL Cabbages will grow in any soil, though the spring cabbages prefer a light soil.

Preparation of Soil Shallow cultivation plus the addition of compost.

Manuring All cabbages need heavy feeding, except the spring cabbage, which, because it has to live through the winter, should not be given too much nitrogen until the spring. A liberal dressing of compost should be used. Use also fish manure at 3 oz to the square yard. During the growing season apply dried blood at 2 oz to the yard run, or old soot used at a handful per yard run.

The ground for cabbages should be well limed if there is a tendency for it to be at all acid : 7-8 oz of hydrated lime should be used to the square yard. This should be applied to the surface of the ground just before the plants are put out.

Seed Sowing The seeds should be sown during the month of July, though in the south it may be preferable to delay the sowing until early in August. Those in doubt should make two small sowings. The seedbed should be prepared as for broccoli and the ground raked down finely, the seed being sown in drills 9 ins apart and $\frac{1}{2}$ in deep. Sow the seed thinly and there is no need to transplant. It should be possible to put the plants out into their permanent positions in September. In the case of the August sowings, planting may be delayed until October.

Planting Out Spring cabbages follow conveniently after such crops as early potatoes, peas or beans, and the manuring for these should be sufficient for the cabbages. The plants should be 18 ins apart and 12 ins between the rows.

General Remarks The stalks of the cabbages should be removed directly they are cut, and be put on the compost heap to rot down as manure. Bash them up with the back of an axe on a chopping block first. If they are left in the ground they will rob the land.

Spring Cabbage. This should not be confused with spring-sown cabbage. Spring cabbages are sown in the summer and planted out in the autumn.

Summer Cabbage Sow the seeds for the summer varieties in March. Further sowings may be made at fourteen day intervals. If this is done, a succession of plants will be provided which may be put out whenever the land is free.

Winter Cabbage Winter cabbage are sometimes preferred to savoys and other 'greens'.

Seed Sowing The seed of the summer varieties may be sown in March. In the south or south-west, two sowings may be made, one in the first week of April and the second early in May. These later sowings are seldom pricked out into further seedbeds, but are sown as for broccoli.

Planting Out The winter cabbage needs plenty of room and so the rows should be 2 ft apart and the plants 2 ft apart in the rows. More compact types may be as close as 18 ins in the rows.

As these plants generally have to be put out during dry weather, watering is advisable. Shallow furrows may be drawn out, and these given a good soaking. The plants may

be 'swished round' in a bucket containing mud and a little lime, and thus the roots become covered with mud and are kept moist. It is surprising what a difference this makes to the recovery of plants. After planting, the rows should be hoed regularly.

General Cultivation Continue hoeing throughout the season. Caterpillars and the blue aphis fly or bug should be anticipated and the plants dusted or sprayed with derris, when an attack is first seen.

Varieties Spring Cabbage: *Clucas First Early Market 218*. One of the earliest varieties of cabbage known, dark green in colour, forming a good heart. *Durham Early*. An earlier variety than First Early, but perhaps not quite as hardy; this forms a very large cabbage indeed. *Flower of Spring*. A compact variety with few outer leaves which produces full-sized hearts of delicate flavour; it seldom bolts. *Harbinger*. A bright, early cabbage; the hearts make delicious eating, and the heads mature early.

Summer Cabbage : In the summer cabbage group there are *very quick maturing* varieties suitable for sowing under cloches or in frames in February, such as : *Velocity*. Round headed, will cut in 12 weeks if not transplanted. *Greyhound*. Pointed heart, moderate firmness. This variety when sown in March and April and covered, can be cut in June and onwards.

Quick maturing varieties are : *Primo*. If sown in March is ready four months later. Firm, tender and excellent flavour. *Fillgap*. A drumhead type which also does well from February or March sowings. Cuts three weeks after Primo. *Emerald Cross*. A large, compact type, uniform, few outer leaves.

September Section : Winnigstadt. A conical variety. Very popular for showing. Remains in condition for a considerable period. *Golden Acre*. A variety to follow Winningstadt, a drumhead of moderate size.

Winter Cabbage : *Autumn Pride*. Throws a drum-like heart, which is firm and of good flavour. A little earlier than January King. *Christmas Drumhead*. A much later variety, it is large, very 'hearty' and needs plenty of room. *January King*. Sown in May, it cuts in February. Extremely hardy.

Red Cabbage (Pickling) : The red cabbage is usually grown for pickling, though in some districts it is stewed. The

The January King cabbage, a photograph taken in August when only half grown. A delicious late cabbage.

epicure insists on it as *the* vegetable for serving with partridge.

Seed Sowing   The seed may be sown in March on a seed-bed. The plants thus raised, when planted out in May should come in for use in the autumn.

Those who require larger heads should sow in the month of August, and these plants will be fit to cut about the same month the following year.

Those who like it stewed may make a sowing in April.

General Cultivation   As for other cabbages.

Varieties   *Early Blood Red*. This is one of the earliest vegetables and should be sown in the spring. Not so large as some. Is a good variety for the north. *Lydiate*. One of the largest red varieties known; it throws a firm heart; it is late and quite hardy.

One of the best of the summer cabbages, Primo is firm-hearted and takes up little room.

Carrots

It should be possible to have carrots as a vegetable all the year round. The main crops may be stored and used as desired in the winter, while sowings of 'frame' varieties give delicious roots very early in the spring. There are many kinds that can be grown, and these may roughly be divided into three :

1 The Shorthorns. These produce short roots, and so are wanted for early sowings in warm borders and for shallow soils.

2 The Intermediate, which are much liked by many people for use as a 'main' crop, especially on the heavier soils.

3 The Long. A type of carrot seldom grown now.

Soil Carrots do best on a deep, well-cultivated sandy loam. Heavy soils may be improved by the addition of sandy material, and on such soils the shorter-rooted types are grown.

Preparation of Soil All root crops like fine pulverized soil. If carrots are to grow with straight, clean roots the soil should not be 'cloddy'.

Sand and even burnt soil will do much to improve the texture of heavy land as will, of course, properly-made compost.

Manuring Carrots do not require large quantities of compost dug into the soil prior to seed sowing. For the early crops use 2 oz of fish manure to the square yard, plus liquid seaweed manure applied at fortnightly intervals, should the growth not be considered quick enough.

For main crops use 4 oz of fish manure to the square yard, applied ten days or more before sowing the seed.

Seed Sowing, Earlies Early sowings can be made in sunny south borders and in other warm spots. These can take place in March in drills 9 ins apart. The rows may even be 6 ins apart for very small varieties. Protection may be given to these beds by using cloches or access frames. It is difficult to ensure germination unless the soil is warm.

Seed Sowing (Main Crop) The seed may be sown in April onwards in drills $\frac{3}{4}$ ins deep and 12 to 15 ins apart, according to the variety. Some gardeners like to mix the seed with a little dry earth, or powdery peat, as this makes thin sowing easier to do. After sowing the drills, the soil should be raked over so as to cover the seed and produce a level bed.

Seed Sowing (Late Crop) A further sowing of early

varieties may be made in July, so as to provide tender young roots in the autumn and winter. These sowings should be carried out in exactly the same way as described for the early sowings.

Thinning There is no need to thin the early sowings providing a really thin sowing is carried out. The roots should be pulled early, when the roots are young. The same holds good with regard to the July sowings. The main crops, however, should be thinned out 4 ins apart, depending on the variety. It is usual to thin at two periods, the first thinning to be done to half the distance required and the second thinning to the final distance. It is during these thinnings that the greatest care should be taken to prevent an attack of carrot fly. Whizzed napthalene should be applied along the rows before thinning and immediately afterwards at 2 ozs to the yard run.

General Cultivation There is little to do other than hoeing to control weeds. Carrot seeds do not germinate properly unless there is sufficient moisture present, and in dry seasons (after sowing the seed) it may be necessary to give the rows a good overhead watering from time to time.

Harvesting Before the autumn and winter frosts appear, the roots should be lifted and stored in sand or dry earth. The tops should be cut off neatly first of all (these being rotted down for compost), and the roots stacked neatly in a shed or a clamp, as described for potatoes. Carrots can be grown in cold frames. In this case the seed is not sown until about mid-February. See that the frame faces south.

Varieties Short Carrots: For Access frames or under cloches or even for catch-crops in the open.

Early Scarlet Horn. Cylindrical, 4 ins long. First class. *Early Gem.* 5 ins long, 3 ins in diameter. Coreless. Oval.

Intermediate or Half-long Carrots (Stump Rooted): *Early Nantes.* Keeps well, medium-sized roots. *Amsterdam Forcing.* Cylindrical, coreless, best of the last carrots for frame growing. *Sweetheart.* Very early, small core, excellent flavour.

Main Crop: *Chantenay.* The most popular main crop half-long type. *New Model Red Cored.* Said to go on growing longer into the autumn than any other variety; 4 to 5 ins long.

Normal Pointed Roots: *James' Scarlet Intermediate.* Small core, bright and clean, one of the most popular varieties, and rightly so. *New Scarlet Intermediate.* Another first-class variety of similar type, long uniform roots.

Long Stump Rooted: *Vita Longa.* Long, heavy stump-rooted, good colour.

Cauliflower

Cauliflowers are one of the most popular summer vegetables and, though they may be likened to the broccoli, they are more delicate in flavour and much in demand.

Soil The cauliflower does best on a loam which has been heavily manured, and whose moisture content is kept up. Whatever the soil may be, it should be liberally fed with compost.

Preparation of Soil The land should be lightly forked and compost incorporated evenly. If the land is covered with compost in the autumn it will be easier to get the soil down into a fine condition in the spring.

Manuring Just before the plants are ready to put out, the ground may be raked over and fish manure added at 3 oz to the square yard. Finally, lime is applied to the surface of the ground.

Seed Sowing There are various times of the year when seed may be sown if an unbroken supply of white curds is aimed at from early June to the end of October.

Autumn Sowing The first sowing should be done in the autumn – round about the middle of August in the northern counties, and early in September in the south. The seeds are sown in warm seed beds outside, and the seedlings thus raised pricked out in quite poor soil into cold frames 4 ins square. Make sure that the seedlings are planted near the glass, so that they do not become drawn. Liberal ventilation may be given throughout the winter on bright days. During the more frosty periods, mats should be used to cover the glass so as to protect the young plants.

When pricking out these young plants, it is most important to see they are not buried. When seedlings are planted too deeply, blind plants result the following summer. The seedlings thus raised can be planted out in March and April in a sheltered part of the garden.

January and February Sowings Those who do not find it convenient to sow in the autumn may raise suitable plants from sowings made in January or early February. In this case the seeds are usually sown in boxes, and these are put out into a greenhouse with sufficient heat on to keep out any frost. When the young seedlings come through, the plants are pricked out as before, this time into light, rich soil. The plants thus raised are usually ready to put out early in April.

The advantage of such a method of sowing is that all worries of over-wintering are eliminated, but the disadvantage is that the crops produced are never as large as those from autumn sowings.

Spring Sowings The seed of the later varieties are sown in March or early April in specially prepared seedbeds out of doors. The seed rows may be 6 ins apart, and when the plants are through they may be thinned out to 3 ins apart, the seedlings being transplanted into further seedbeds if necessary. These seedbeds should be watered regularly if dry, to get the plants growing, and should also be hoed regularly.

Later Sowings Still later sowings may be made late in April or early in May. Here again the seeds are sown out of doors in a fine seedbed, and the young plants thus raised planted out when they are fit to handle, in rows 6 ins apart with 3 ins between the plants. The late cropping varieties are chosen for this purpose.

Planting Out The autumn sowings are planted out in early March in the south in a sheltered situation, the plants being 1 ft square. On a very rich soil it may be necessary to plant them 18 ins by 1 ft. For the later sowings, the distance between the rows may be increased to 2 ft, the plants being 18 ins apart in the rows. It much depends on soil, climate, and the manuring whether these greater distances are necessary or not. For the late summer sowings the rows may be as far apart as $2\frac{1}{2}$ ft, the cauliflowers being 2 ft between the plants.

Planting should always be done firmly. The hole should be made large enough for this to be done. The plants should be planted out before they become too big, and better crops will result.

General Cultivation Hoeing between the plants is necessary, and during dry weather you must give copious waterings. This is very necessary, especially in the early stages, for no check in the growth must occur if you are to get large curds.

Should the weather be warm when the plants are curd-

**Cauliflower
Dobies Snowdrift**

Carters

ing, one or two of the inner leaves may be bent over the 'flower' to prevent it from opening up or turning yellow. It is quite easy to break the centre vein of a leaf without severing the leaf altogether.

It is to be hoped that the season will not be too dry, but if it is, and the plants need water, heavy drenchings by means of an overhead sprinkler are necessary. These should always be followed by a good hoeing.

Harvesting The curds should be cut as early in the morning as possible, and brought into the house while they are still wet with dew. In cases where too many heads become ready to cut at one time, whole plants may be pulled up with soil attached to the roots, and these may be hung in a shed, upside-down, and used as desired.

Varieties (a) For sowing in the autumn and planting out in April for cutting in early June. *Cluseed Major.* A good all round type; the largest curd; sow in September. *All the Year Round.* Sow early September; neat compact growth. *Unwin's Snowflake.* Good medium size, close white curds. (b) For sowing mid-February, for cutting mid-June early July. *Leader.* Withstands drought better than any other type. *Unwin's Snocap.* Quick growing, very early, very compact. *King of Cauliflowers.* Dwarf, medium size. *Early Snowball.* Forms a close, white curd; small to medium size. (c) For sowing in March to crop in August and early September. *Majestic.* Very large and fine type of cauliflower. *Early September.* One of the earliest large-headed; comes into use early in September; good quality. (d) For sowing in April to crop in October, November. *Veitch's Autumn Giant.* Produces huge white heads of excellent quality. *Dominant.* Very well protected, pure white heads; a first-class variety.

Celery

Celery is an excellent vegetable to grow because it is health-giving, especially to older people. This is one of the vegetables that can be used either as a salad or when cooked.

Soil The main requirement for celery is that the soil should be deep. Many market gardeners prefer peaty soil for celery production, because of the high amount of organic matter present. Acid soils seem to grow better celery than those that have a high lime content. A soil which retains moisture easily is important, because plants have a tendency to go to seed if they receive a check owing to dryness at the roots.

Preparation of Soil This consists principally in preparing special trenches in which the celery is grown. Normally these are prepared 16 ins deep and 18 ins wide, but the compost grower can have them as shallow as 6 ins deep and 12 ins wide. Celery should NOT be planted deeply, especially on heavy soils, but the use of a trench makes it easier to blanch the celery subsequently, and to ensure that the plants receive sufficient moisture throughout their growing season.

The soil is taken out carefully when the trenches are being prepared and is then thrown on either side of the trench in equal proportions, and this makes ridges of equal height.

The ridges made at the sides of the trenches should be flattened, and catch-crops can be grown on these if desired. Lettuces, radishes and shallots are most suitable for this purpose. The earlier the trenches are dug the earlier can the ridges be used for growing a catch-crop.

Manuring Use well-rotted compost and fill the bottom of the trench with this so that it is at least 3 ins deep when trodden down firmly. On this a 1-in depth of good friable soil should be placed.

In addition to the large quantity of organic matter placed in the bottom of the trench, regular 'feeds' will be given with liquid manure. This can be purchased ready for dilution and when diluted is poured into the trench every ten days or so with a watering can.

Seed Sowing Beginners are apt to sow seeds too early, and as a result the plants tend to bolt (i.e. throw up a flower stem) during the summer. The earliest seed to be sown should be about the middle of February, and from such sowings good sticks should be ready to use late in August and at the beginning of September. These earlier sowings are made in boxes, and a compost rich in organic matter is used. Celery seeds on the whole germinate readily, and so thin sowing is necessary. After the seeds are sown, a little of a similar compost may be sifted over them and the soil pressed down lightly with a wooden presser.

The boxes are then put in the greenhouse at a temperature of 60 to 65 degrees F. They may be covered with a sheet of glass on top of which is placed a piece of brown paper. Once the seeds have germinated, the glass and paper should be removed and the boxes set on a shelf near the light. A fortnight or so later the seedlings may be pricked out into further boxes, placing them 3 ins apart. This time a slightly 'heavier' compost may be used.

Main Sowing The main sowing is usually carried out early in March, in boxes in the greenhouse as before. Celery seeds do not germinate quickly, but once they have, the plants will grow steadily. When they are 2 ins high they may be transplanted. The advantage of these various times of sowing for those who are particularly fond of celery is that a constant supply may be achieved from the end of August to the following March. Those who have no greenhouse may carry out the sowings in frames, or under cloches.

Planting Out When the plants are ready, they may be planted out into the trenches. At this time they will usually be 3 or 4 ins high. The plants are lifted carefully with a trowel and then planted in the trenches 1 ft apart. Some gardeners have them as close as 9 ins, and this smaller distance may be sufficient for the weaker-growing varieties. After planting, the soil is made firm around them and then the trench is given a thorough soaking with water and the soil at the bottom of the trench hoed thoroughly the next day.

General Cultivation During the whole of the growing season the trenches must be kept moist by regular waterings. These waterings will probably alternate with the feeds of liquid manure outlined in the paragraph dealing with manuring. Throughout the season the ridges should be kept hoed; the catch-crops should be harvested when ready.

Any side-growths that come from the base of the celery plants should be removed. These suckers only rob the main plant and are of no value. The plants should be sprayed regularly with nicotine and soft soap to keep down celery fly, and if necessary with Bordeaux Mixture for the prevention of celery leaf spot, also known as celery blight.

During the winter it is necessary to protect celery from frost. There are one or two ways of doing this. The tops may be covered with straw or bracken, or the tops may be bent slightly to one side at the last earthing so as to prevent the moisture from trickling down into the heart of the plant during a sunny or rainy period.

On the other hand, during the summer celery benefits from having the foliage sprinkled every day during the hot weather. This should be done late in the afternoon.

Earthing-Up In order that celery may be fit to eat it must be blanched, and this may be done at regular intervals; it is not advisable to earth higher than the base of the leaves.

It is usual to do the first earthing-up with the handfork and to bring the soil up to the base of the plant in a 'loose manner', which allows the plant to expand. All that is necessary is to bring some earth half way up the plant and all round it.

The earthing-up should always be done with the hand grasped firmly around the plant while the soil is put into position. Avoid allowing any soil to get in between the stems. The first proper earthing-up is done when the plants are over 1 ft high. This may be about the middle of August. Another earthing is carried out three weeks later, and the final earthing some time during the month of October. It is at this last earthing that the soil is brought up to the top of the stem as high as the bottom leaves. When earthing-up, the ridges should be made smooth and steep as in this way the rain is carried away and does not get down into the plants.

Wrap the celery plants with brown paper or corrugated cardboard. This is tied into position and prevents soil from reaching the stems. Loose ties can always be made if necessary, and some gardeners use wide rubber bands, which they slip up the plant as the earthing-up process proceeds.

Reiteration It may be as well to reiterate some of the important points in celery production, and they are as follows : Grow the plants slowly, without any check. Always arrange for plenty of organic matter to allow a free root run. Be on the lookout all the time for celery fly, especially when the plants are in the frame. Thoroughly spray with nicotine whenever necessary. Earthing-up so as to blanch; and if the beginner finds it difficult to hold the plant with one hand while he is pushing the soil around it with the other, another helper may grasp around the plant with both hands. Another method is to put a loose tie of raffia round each plant. Earthing-up should never be carried out when the plants or the soil are wet.

Harvesting About eight weeks should be allowed after the first earthing-up before the sticks are sufficiently

The Greensleeves variety of green celery does not need any earthing up at all and is delicious.

blanched to be used in the house. When the necessary period has elapsed, the celery stick may be dug up from the trench, the soil being placed around the dug-up portion so as to prevent the sticks on either side from greening.

Varieties White : *Exhibition.* Popular because it is fairly resistant to septoria blight. Is crisp and of good flavour. Pink : *Superb Pink.* An old and heavy winter celery. Though truly a pink it blanches nearly white. The stem is very wide at the base and hardly tapers up to the foliage. Red : *Standard Bearer.* Throws very solid sticks of good size and flavour. *Exhibition.* An excellent flavoured red-coloured variety. Excellent for table use.

Celery, Self-Blanching

Celery, Self-Blanching Those who have not the room for trenches, or do not care for one reason or another to prepare them, should concentrate on growing celery on the flat, choosing one of the self-blanching varieties – or one of the new green eating varieties (as Greensleeves).

The soil where this crop is to be grown should be forked lightly, and enriched with plenty of finely divided compost. The celery plants, which can be raised in the ordinary way, are then planted out in rows 18 ins apart, the plants being 1 ft apart in the rows. The Greensleeves should be 18 ins by 18 ins. When the plants are put out on the flat, the ground should be well soaked afterwards, and the following day the bed should be lightly hoed over.

Though the celery is called 'self-blanching', it is usually necessary to place some straw among the plants in order to ensure that the stems are really white. It is possible in small gardens to blanch each individual plant by tying stiff paper collars into position. In the case of the Greensleeves there is nothing to do as the celery is delicious when the stems are green.

Varieties *Lathom Blanching.* Crisp and nutty, free from strings. *Golden Self-Blanching.* Probably the best pure white dwarf. Has an excellent flavour. *Greensleeves.* The light green stems are meaty-crisp and nutty.

Kale

The kales, though not perhaps the most delicious of vegetables, are invaluable because they are so hardy and ensure a good supply of green vegetables throughout the winter months. The kales as a whole are improved by frosts.

Soil There is no need to worry about special soil condition, as kales will grow well in practically all gardens.

Preparation of Soil There is no need to make special preparations, as they usually follow a well-manured crop *Russian Kale. This very* and are quite content with the soil preparation and *hardy breed thrives* manuring given to that previous crop.
through any winter. **Manuring** See Cabbage.

Seed Sowing It should be possible to make a sowing of seed during the first week of March in the south, and towards the end of March in the north. Further sowings can be made during the second and third weeks of April. A fine seedbed should be prepared by raking the soil down well, and if an open situation can be chosen, so much the better.

The drills should be 9 ins apart, and if the plants are to be thinned and transplanted they should be put out 6 ins apart in the rows. Asparagus kale may be sown as late as June and July.

Transplanting Should the plants become rather large and the rows somewhat crowded, it is possible to transplant the young plants into further seedbeds. If this is done, stouter, firmer plants are produced; and these give a better crop in the long run. The final transplanting into their permanent positions is usually done towards the end of June or the beginning of July onwards. They are a very useful crop to follow early potatoes, early peas, or even French beans.

General Cultivation When the plants are put out, they must have plenty of water to start with. This can be achieved by puddling the plants in.

Harvesting Kales may be harvested as desired, but it is inadvisable to use them until the other green vegetables are scarce. In this way they are able to grow unrestricted and build up a good plant. Early in the new year the heads of the kales may be removed, and in this way dozens of side-growths will break out. These prove very useful.

Varieties *Hardy Sprouting.* A type that will withstand the most rigorous weather. Large shoots are produced all down the main stem. They are delicious. *Dwarf Green Curled.* A kale which is robust and compact in growth. The leaves are densely curled. A very hardy variety. *Asparagus kale.* One of the later varieties. Hardy, producing as it does, a large number of shoots in the spring. Is sometimes sown where the crop is intended to be grown. *Thousand-headed.* A very hardy variety which is strong and branching in habit. Is excellent for use in the spring. *Russian kale.* Extremely hardy. Produces dense head of foliage in November and then abundant delicious young shoots in the spring. *Hungry Gap kale.* Withstands drought, wet and frost. Very late and hardy. Sow where it is to grow. *Variegated Kales.* Extremely decorative, ranging from Ivory-white to bright rose and crimson. Colour disappears in cooking.

Leek

The leek is essentially a northern vegetable. Has become more popular year by year, because even the severest of winters cannot harm the plants.

Soil Leeks can be grown on practically all soils. They naturally prefer a well drained loam, and do not like a very light sand. Leeks like soil in which there is plenty of organic matter present. They prefer soils that retain moisture readily.

Preparation of Soil The best results may be obtained by growing leeks in trenches as has been described for celery. The compost should be forked into the bottom of the trench and 1 in of good soil put on top of this. This leaves the trenches about 6 ins deep. Plant the leeks in the trenches 1 ft apart.

Manuring The compost that is forked into the bottom of the trench will be the main requirement of this crop. Many growers like to use a little dried poultry manure as well, and they apply this along the rows at the rate of about 1 oz to the yard run.

Those who cannot obtain poultry manure should use 2 oz of fish manure per yard run instead, once a month, or dried bood may be given at the rate of 2 oz per yard run. If leeks are grown on the flat the same kind of manurial dressings should be given.

Seed Sowing The seed may be sown in gentle heat under glass towards the end of January. The No-Soil compost should be used in quite shallow boxes. The seed is sown thinly, a little light soil is sifted over it and it is then pressed down lightly with a wooden presser. Water is given at the same temperature as the house, through a fine rose of a can. The boxes are covered with a sheet of glass and with a piece of brown paper, and after the seedlings have appeared, the glass and paper are removed and the boxes are stood on a shelf near the glass.

When the baby plants are an inch or so high they may be pricked out into other boxes 1 to $1\frac{1}{2}$ ins apart, with more No-Soil compost. The boxes are filled to within $\frac{1}{4}$ in of the top after pressing the soil down evenly and firmly. The boxes are watered, placed on the shelf of the glasshouse, and kept at a temperature of about 55 degrees F.

When these plants are growing well, at 5 or 6 ins high, they should be hardened off gradually, by placing them in a cold frame. This usually takes place towards the end of March. By airing the frames regularly it should be possible to remove the lights by the third week of April, when the leeks can be planted out.

A sowing may be made in the open about the third week of March – the rows should be 18 ins apart and the seeds sown thinly. Later, thin the plants to 9 ins, and use the thinnings for planting out.

Planting Out The plants should be taken out of the soil very carefully so as not to break the roots. If a large ball of soil can be retained around them, so much the better. Should it be necessary to break the roots when planting out, the foliage should be cut back to help balance things up.

The plants should be given a thorough watering-in, and,

Hoeing between newly planted leeks.
Leeks planted 'on the flat', not in trenches.

in fact, leeks will benefit from regular waterings once a week, especially during dry weather. Further, those who are keen on producing a perfect leek will syringe the plants overhead in the evening at the end of a hot day. Liquid manure can be given, as suggested for celery, from time to time.

Those who have not the time or the inclination to prepare trenches for leeks may grow them in rows 1 ft apart, the plants being 8 ins apart in the rows. Holes are made with a dibber 9 ins deep and the leeks are dropped into the bottom of the hole after the leaves are cut back by half. These holes are not filled in, but the plants soon secure root hold, especially if a little water is poured into the holes after planting.

Yet another method of planting is to make drills 9 ins apart and 6 ins deep and to put the young leek plants out in these at 8 ins apart.

General Cultivation Hoeing will be necessary to keep the ground clean. If any flower-stems appear, these should be nipped out immediately. From time to time, as the plants develop in the trenches, soil may be placed around the stems so as to blanch them. It is quite possible to start blanching 3 weeks after planting and to continue by placing a little finely-broken-up soil around the stems once a fortnight. Blanching may be done by means of stiff brown paper, and in some gardens, agricultural drain pipes 2½ ins in diameter are used.

The advantage of using brown paper or corrugated cardboard for leeks is that it does prevent the soil getting in between the leaves, and it is this grittiness of leeks when they appear on the table that so often puts people off.

Harvesting The leeks may be dug up as required, the soil being put back in position so as to keep the other stems white.

Varieties *The Lyon.* The leeks used more for exhibition purposes than any other variety. Solid and compact. *Marble Pillar.* A medium green variety with long white stems. Very suitable for the north. A long leek. *Walter Mammoth.* A type with very dark green leaves and enormous stems. Of first class flavour. *Giant Musselburgh.* A midland-northern and Scottish variety with long thick pure white stems. *Everest.* One of the largest leeks known, excellent for show or table use.

Lettuce

There is no doubt that the lettuce is the most popular of all salad crops. It is possible, by careful management, to ensure having crisp hearts all the year round, if frames, cloches and greenhouse are used. There are two main groups, the cos and the cabbage lettuce, but for the winter it is the cabbage varieties that are principally grown.

Few people realize that lettuces can be cooked in the same way as cabbage, and taste similar to spinach. One of the best ways to prepare them for the table is to parboil them first and then to simmer them in milk.

Soil The soil for lettuce should be rich in organic material. This ensures that the moisture is retained during the warmer months. On the whole a light, rich soil is preferable, especially if this is liberally manured.

Preparation of Soil It is here where the good gardener can score, as he will fork in large quantities of well-rotted compost shallowly. In addition, he will use organic forms of fertilizers, such as fish or meat or bone, in the top 2 ins, lightly forked in.

Manuring The advice given in the previous paragraph should be borne in mind. It is as well to give lettuce a dressing consisting of 2 oz fine fish manure, $\frac{1}{2}$ oz of bone meal and 4 oz of wood ashes. Two oz of dried blood may be applied to the square yard as a top-dressing and lightly hoed in, a week or ten days before the plants are due to heart.

Seed Sowing Lettuce may be sown at various times of the year, both in the open and under glass.

Spring Sowings From the beginning of March onwards it is possible to make sowings of lettuce at fortnightly intervals until the middle of April, and at three weekly intervals from the middle of April until the beginning of August. The plants raised from these sowings may either be allowed to grow where they are sown, or may be thinned out and transplanted to further borders.

The drills for the earliest sowings are usually 6 ins apart, and as soon as the young seedlings appear they are thinned out to 6 ins apart. The sowings that are done in the open for growing where they are sown should be made in rows 1 ft apart, the plants being thinned to 10 ins apart. Even in such a case, any thinnings that are required may be transplanted.

August Sowings During the third week in August in the

south, and about the second week in August in the north, it is possible to sow seed thinly on a specially prepared, moist seedbed. It is here where the use of sedge peat comes in handy. Use this at half a 2-gallon bucketful to the square yard. Special varieties are used for such sowings, and the plants thus raised are put out in rows 1 ft apart, and 10 ins apart in the rows.

Again, it is possible to sow the rows where the lettuces are to grow, and to thin the plants out to 5 ins before the winter sets in. A second thinning to 10 ins may be carried out in the spring.

Thinning and Transplanting It is practically impossible except by the single-seed-sowing method, to guarantee that lettuces are sown thinly enough. Many gardeners affirm that lettuces cannot be thinned and transplanted too early.

Lettuces must be given plenty of room to develop, and kept growing quickly, and a crisp appetizing salad results. It is those that are crowded, and so are slow in growth, that end to be "soft" and unpalatable.

Lettuces should be handled carefully, as they are tender and can easily be damaged. The roots also dry out quickly, and for this reason they should not be left out of the soil longer than necessary. They must not be transplanted deeply, as otherwise 'peaky' plants result, but should, however, be planted firmly. If the land is at all dry there is a danger of botrytis.

General Cultivation The hoe must be kept going between the rows. It is not advisable to go on to the land in the winter, but even under these conditions, when the soil is warm enough, surface cultivation will do a great deal of good.

Cos lettuces do not heart naturally as easily as the cabbage varieties, and for this reason they are often tied round with raffia when they have made three-quarters of their growth in order to help them to heart properly. The cos lettuces too, seem to need far more moisture, and so should be regularly watered.

Harvesting Lettuces should be cut as soon as they are ready. If they are not, they will quickly go to seed, and then are of little value except for cooking.

Variety Classification The two main groups of lettuce are, of course, (a) the Cabbage and (b) the Cos, but in addition there is an Intermediate type generally known as the Density Group, the best of which is perhaps Little Gem. It is important to know which type and variety to sow at differing periods of the year. It is important also to realize that certain types of lettuce prefer the short days of the winter and so do well under glass while others insist on the long days of summer and thus do better during the summer months.

Varieties (a) Heated greenhouse or frame for growing in the winter. *Cheshunt Early Giant.* Raised by the Research Station for the heated frame, but does not do badly in unheated frames. *Blackpool.* A light green lettuce, ideal for frames, especially in the north. Quite good for cloches also. *Loos Tennis Ball.* A slow growing looser-leaved type of lettuce, popular in the north. Is said to be immune from mildew.

(b) Varieties for the unheated greenhouse in winter and the cold frame. May do well from spring sowings in the open. *May Queen.* Sometimes called 'May King.' Insist on a good strain. Produces a large lettuce with a good heart, loves air. *Attractie.* May be the best cloche or Ganwick lettuce. *Hilde.* A medium green type; hearts well. Larger than Attractie.

(c) Varieties for sowing in September, for cutting in November or for sowing in October for standing the winter in the open. *Imperial Winter.* Produces a solid heart of good size, hardy, probably the best of the clear green leaved type. *Arctic King.* Much recommended but really much too small. Is of good quality and very hardy.

(d) A variety that only succeeds when sown in the autumn for standing out of doors in the winter and cutting in the spring. *McHatties Giant.* A good old-fashioned type with large spreading puckered leaves and a loosish heart. Though hardy is apt to be coarse.

(e) Varieties for sowing very early in spring, for cutting in the spring, for cutting out of doors. *Borough Wonder.* A good lettuce with solid heart of a pleasant colour. Stands drought well. Leaves pale green. *Unrivalled Trocadero Improved.* The original type of this group, hardy. Medium to large well-shaped heads.

(f) Varieties for sowing in spring and summer but which are not hardy. *All the Year Round.* Firm heart, well flavoured medium dark green puckered leaves. *Cornell 456.* Has large light green leaves, crumpled and crisp in character, but a particularly good variety for dry soils, beautiful flavour. *Continuity.* An excellent variety for those who do not mind the brownish or purpley leaves. Produces a good tender heart.

(g) Varieties with the crisp curled leaves known as 'Iceberg.' Sown any time during the spring or summer. *Webb's Wonderful.* Perhaps the best of the group. Grows really large with waxy green foliage.

(h) The Gathering Group, to be sown any time during the spring or summer. Should never be transplanted. *Salad Bowl.* Loose, crisp curled leaves which may be picked like spinach – or the whole lettuce may be cut to become the base of the salad bowl.

Cos Lettuces (a) Summer type: *Paris White.* May be sown in the autumn in frames and with some protection will then stand the winter. Best all-round variety. Dark green, self folding, large. *Balloon.* Its name suggests what it looks like when growing. Has big outer leaves that enclose the heart with balloon-like effect.

(b) Density Group: *Winter Density.* Glossy dark green leaves, hardy, very delicious. Lovely firm, semi-cos hearts. *Little Gem.* Perhaps the best strain of this group. May be sown in spring as well as in the autumn. Delicious yellow hearts, firm and tender. Sometimes called 'Sugar Cos'.

Marrow

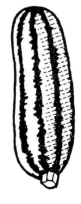

The marrow is the vegetable crop that is often grown on the rubbish heap and in any odd corner of the garden. Many people do not realize that it may be grown up a fence, a shady one being most suitable for the purpose. It may also, of course, be grown in its bush form in rows like any other vegetable.

During wet years the marrow will appreciate being grown on a mound, because its roots will be drier, but in dry years it likes growing on the flat.

Soil Marrow can be grown on almost any soil, providing they are (a) well drained, and (b) rich in organic material.

Preparation of Soil If this crop can follow one which has been liberally manured, then there is little special cultivation to be done. Crops that are harvested in May usually leave the land in a good condition for marrows.

Manuring As much organic material as possible should be incorporated shallowly into the soil where the marrows are to grow. Some gardeners make furrows 2 ins deep and fill these with well-decayed compost. They tread this down well and then replace the soil, forming a ridge over the compost or manure. In this way a certain amount of bottom heat is generated, and the plants start growing quickly.

In addition, a fish manure or meat and bone meal should be forked in a fortnight before planting at 3 oz to the square yard.

Seed Sowing It is possible to sow the seeds outside in a little pocket of specially prepared soil where the plants are to grow. This is especially true of the rubbish heap, where little soil pockets may be made at intervals. In this case it is advisable to cover these pockets with a glass jam-jar, in order to help germination and give the seedlings some protection when they come through. Don't sow the seed much before the first week of May. The plants raised in this way will be later in cropping than those raised under glass.

Under Glass It is usual to sow seeds in 3 in pots which are filled with No-Soil compost.

The plants raised in pots are hardened off, the ones in the greenhouse being taken out into frames, and the ones in frames being given more and more air. In this way they should be quite ready to be put out in the open ground during the third week of May. Even in the greenhouse the greatest care should be taken not to over-water.

Planting Out Where numbers of marrows are to be grown, the rows should be set out 3 ft apart, and the plants in the rows set 3 ft apart. Bush marrows are preferable for this system.

When growing 'trailers' these may be kept pinched back, or they may be planted on the rubbish heap or any similar corner and allowed to ramble as they like. They can also be trained up wires fixed to a wall or fence.

General Cultivation Marrows that are grown in the rows should be hoed, and, in order to conserve moisture and to increase the crop, mulchings may be given with sedge peat or compost during June. It is worth while pollinating marrow flowers in the early part of the season with a camel's-hair brush.

Harvesting Marrows should be cut when they are young and tender. If they are they are not only more delicious, but the plants will produce a heavier crop. It is said that regular cutting may treble the crop.

Varieties *Long White.* A long white trailing type, bearing

Unwins

Jan King
'January King', a hardy winter cabbage

Carters

Lettuce
The most valuable all-round salad

Carters

Onion
Showmaster

Unwins

Runner Bean
Hammonds

a large smooth marrow with no rib or neck. *Long Green.* A very prolific type of marrow. Dark in colour and ideal for the table. *Bush-shaped Green.* Bears medium-sized fruits, bright green in colour, early in the season. *Bush-shaped White.* Similar to the previous variety, but the fruits are of a beautiful creamy-white colour. *Zucchini.* Bears long deep emerald green fruits of excellent table quality with a delicate flavour.

Onion

The onion has been used as a food longer than almost any other vegetable. Two hundred years before the birth of Christ it was written about, and it is known that the Pharaohs had it on their tables. There is a constant demand for onions. The main reason why it is not cultivated more is because few people know how to keep down the ravages of the onion fly.

Soil Onions prefer a sandy, rich loam. Onions, however, will grow in heavy clay soils providing these can be 'opened up' by adding sand, burnt soil or even plenty of powdery compost.

Preparation of Soil It is the preparation of the soil that is more important than the soil itself, for most soils may be improved. Some growers try to obtain clay for their sandy soils, while others with heavier textured soils fork in sand. Having added the necessary 'ingredients', the soil should be forked lightly so as to make it fine and loose.

The soil should be well drained and yet contain sufficient organic material to retain moisture. Onions can be grown on the same soil year after year. It is usual to make the surface of the soil firm before sowing the seed and this can be done by a very light rolling, or by treading. This firming should never be done when the soil is 'pasty' but may be done directly the weather improves.

Manuring When preparing the soil, 5 cwt of well-rotted compost can be used to the square pole. Poultry manure or fish manure can be used as a top dressing – 3 ozs to the square yard, a week or so before planting. Wood ashes may also be used if they are available, at the rate of $\frac{1}{2}$-lb to the square yard.

During the growing season, dried blood may be used as a tonic from time to time at 1 oz per yard to nourish the plants.

Onions, Spring Sown SEED SOWING The spring-sown

onion is one that is harvested in the autumn, and should not, therefore, be called as it sometimes is, the spring onion. When the soil is in the right condition – that is, the top $\frac{1}{2}$-in or so should be almost dry – the soil may be consolidated and the little drills prepared. It is possible in the south to do this during the month of March, and in the north very often in April. In the south-west I have seen onions sown in January.

The seed should be sown in rows 1 ft apart and the drills should be very shallow. To cover these drills up it should only be necessary to do a little light raking, and finally a treading along the rows to firm the soil to ensure its contact with the seed. Again, this firming should not be done if the soil is inclined to be sticky.

General Cultivation Directly the seeds have germinated and the crop is visible, hoeing should commence, and it should be remembered with onions that hoeing should tend to be away from the rows and not up with them. A few weeks later the rows should be possible to thin, and an attempt should be made to leave little groups 3 ins apart. The intermediate groups will be thinned out a few weeks later, and the onions thus pulled should supply material for salad. Finally the little groups will be thinned down to one plant, which should produce a good bulb.

When an onion is growing properly, it should sit on the surface of the soil, and thus receive the benefit of the rays of the sun. If the earth is drawn up to onion bulbs, they tend to elongate. It is during this thinning process that the onion fly has an opportunity of laying eggs, and so starting the maggots on their career. To prevent this, a little whizzed napthalene should be sprinkled between the rows.

On light land and during a hot dry summer it may be necessary to water, giving a good soaking when necessary. This watering should be discontinued about the middle of August, so as to allow the bulbs to ripen.

Harvesting The bulbs should ripen naturally, but to help them the tops are usually bent over at the neck. After this, the necks will commence to shrink, and 10–14 days later, the onions may be lifted out of the soil and left on the surface of the ground to dry off. This drying-off process may be continued by taking the bulbs, shaking any earth off that may cling to the roots, and laying them on a gravel or cinder path in the sun.

After this the onions may be stored in a cool, dry, airy place. It is possible to hang them up in ropes under the shelter of the eaves of a building, or on the walls of a potting or tool shed. The main thing is not to allow them to get damp, as otherwise they tend to start growing again. *Onions, Autumn Sown* It is possible to sow onions in the autumn either to produce salad onions in the spring or to produce fair-sized bulbs the following summer. Different varieties are chosen for these two purposes.

Seed Sowing The seed is sown either during the latter part of July or during the middle of August, depending on the situation of the garden – the further north the earlier the sowing. The rows may be 9 ins apart for the salad onions and 12 ins apart for the onions that are to bulb.

The sowing of such onions usually follows the harvesting of a well-manured crop, and it is only necessary to rake ground finely, draw out the drills, and then sow thinly.

General Cultivation Hoeing is carried out and continued until the winter makes this impossible, and then in the spring regular cultivations may commence again. In the case of the salad onions no thinning is done, as the plants are pulled out as required. The varieties that are to bulb are often thinned, and the thinnings are transplanted in the spring 12 ins between the rows and 6 to 9 ins between the plants.

Many people prefer autumn-sown onions, as they are not attacked in the same way by the onion fly, and, in the north, where the spring-sown onion does not get the chance of ripening off properly, the autumn sown varieties prove advantageous.

Onion Sets It is an advantage to use onion sets on soil where onion seed will not germinate easily, and where attacks of the onion fly are particularly bad. To obtain good onion sets carry out the following directions.

Sow the seed in the middle of May to early June in a seed bed of well consolidated soil, with a fine tilth and of good water holding capacity, these conditions are essential. The seeds should be sown in drills $\frac{1}{2}$-in deep and marked out with a rake with teeth 1 in apart. It is found that the seed is sown more evenly by this method than if broadcast. Sown at the rate of $\frac{1}{2}$-oz per square yard a good proportion of usable sets is produced. No thinning is necessary.

Be sure the sets are fully matured before lifting, as early

lifting encourages bolting next season. Too large sets are also apt to bolt. Aim to get them $\frac{1}{4}$ in to $\frac{3}{4}$ in diameter.

Dry off thoroughly in an airy greenhouse, clean and store on wire bottomed trays in a warm temperature, if possible, as this helps to prevent bolting.

Plant out at the end of March in drills 1 in deep and 12 ins apart, with 6–8 ins between the sets. The ground should be prepared as for spring-sown onions. Heavy applications of nitrogenous manures are not advised as they do not make very small sets grow into large bulbs, but produce bulbs liable to neck rot.

Onions, Pickling SOIL Little preparation of the soil is necessary.

Seed Sowing The seed is usually broadcast over the surface of the soil and this is lightly raked in. This should be done in April; the crop is not thinned and, providing the weeds are kept down, excellent little pickling bulbs will be formed. When the seeds are sown shallowly the bulbs are round, but those who prefer long or oval-shaped bulbs should sow the seed 1 in deep.

Varieties 1 Autumn sowers for bulbing. This group produces bulbs which do not keep well but a supply of earlier bulbs in the season is assured. Sow in August or September

Boxing up onions grown organically from onion sets.

for harvesting the following June and do not attempt to keep them after Christmas. *Giant Rocca.* A flattish-oval type of mild flavour, stout, stiffish light green leaves. *White Tripoli.* A mild delicious onion but not a good keeper. *Red Wethersfield.* Sometimes called Red Italian, has a red outer skin and a white skin inside tinged with red at the margin.

2 Autumn sowing for pulling as a spring or salad onion. *White Lisbon.* The favourite silver-skin variety for pulling green for salads. Subject to disease. *White Portugal.* Really one of the white Spanish type but often used as a salad onion.

3 The oval onion. Seldom seen in this country except at Shows, but comes very true from seed. *Coconut.* Its name suggest its shape. Has a strawy brown outer-skin and white flesh. Keeps well.

4 Spanish or Portugal Onion   Normally sown in the spring out of doors for harvesting in the late autumn. *James Keeping.* A strong flavoured variety which keeps well throughout the winter. *Wijbo.* Perfect ball shape, heavy cropper. *Ailsa Craig.* An excellent keeper. Globe-shaped, golden straw colour. *Improved Reading.* Straw coloured skin, large bulbs, mild flavour, juicy solid white flesh. *Nuneham Park.* Another similar type which is difficult to distinguish from Reading.

5 The Dutch Onion includes all the best Exhibition varieties known. The exhibition types have their seeds sown in January, under glass, but normally the varieties are sown in the spring for harvesting in the autumn. *Crossling's Selected.* Probably the largest strain of this group known. Is used by the winners at most shows. The seed, however, is not easy to obtain. *The Premier.* Another Exhibitor's variety of pale straw colour. Grows to an immense size. *Unwin's Exhibition.* Produces large bulbs which should be oblong in shape, tapering to the neck. Often unbeatable on the Show Bench. *Bedfordshire Champion.* One of the most popular varieties. Keeps well. Flesh white and mild. Skin strawy brown. *Unwin's Reliance.* May be a hybrid but fits in here best. Will keep till May. Crops heavily with hard bulbs, mild in flavour. Is conical in shape with slightly rounded base. Best sown in the autumn.

6 Pickling   *Barla.* Small pure white globe-shaped. Matures at the end of July. *The Queen.* Silver-skinned, small, delicious.

Parsnip

The parsnip is one of the easiest of all vegetables to grow, and one that is the least popular. Perhaps the reason for its unpopularity is that it is seldom cooked properly, but when it is baked in beef dripping, or fried after it has been part-boiled, it is particularly delicious. Even when boiled properly, so that it is like 'a mass of marrow', and covered with a white sauce it takes some beating.

Soil The parsnip will grow in any soil providing it is not too stony. Those who have difficulty in getting long, straight roots may bore holes 3 ft deep and 3 ins in diameter at the top. These holes are filled up with friable sifted soil and three seeds are sown on the top. When the seedlings grow they are thinned out so as to leave one in position, and the result is a very large, straight, clean root.

Preparation of Soil The soil is shallowly forked so as to get it into a good friable condition. Fork or rake the ground down in February or March ready for sowing the seed.

Manuring Parsnips should be grown on land that was manured well the previous year, and, if the land is thought to be poor, fertilizers may be added, as described for carrots.

Seed Sowing The seeds are sown in the south at the end of February and in the north during the third week in March, providing the land is in the right condition. Parsnip seeds do not germinate as well as many others, and so the seed should be sown thickly. The rows should be 18 ins apart and 1 in deep.

Thinning When the seedlings are an inch or so high, they may be thinned out to 8 ins apart. Some gardeners who want to get their roots to exhibition size should thin their plants to 6 ins and finally to 1 ft apart later on.

General Cultivation There is little else to be done except to hoe to keep down weeds.

Harvesting Parsnips are not damaged by frost; in fact, they improve in flavour after they have been 'touched'. If there is any danger of the soil being frozen hard, so as to prevent the roots from being dug out when required, then a certain number of them may be lifted and stored in soil in a shed or clamp. Other than this, parsnips may be left in the ground until required, and under ordinary conditions a little litter placed over the rows will prevent the soil from being frozen hard.

When the land is required the following February, any roots that remain may be lifted and stored in earth or sand.

Varieties *Improved Hollow Crown.* An excellent variety in the south-east. Produces a heavy crop of long, well-shaped roots. *Tender and True.* A smaller variety, but is said to have a clearer and smoother skin than others. *The Student.* A large variety of good colour. Suitable for the north, where late sowings have to be made. *Avonresister.* Should be grown where the disease canker has given trouble in the past.

Peas

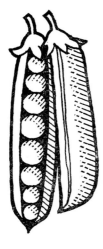

Peas are one of the most popular vegetables, though one in which the supply is so often shortlived, for people fail to realize the necessity of regular sowings to keep up the supply. For this reason detailed suggestions are given in this chapter in the hope that gardeners will be able to keep picking them from July to the end of September.

Like beans, they have nodules on their roots containing bacteria which live in harmony with the plant. These extract nitrogen from the air, and when the roots are left in the ground after the plants are cleared, much natural nitrogenous plant food is added to the soil.

Soil It is possible to grow peas on most soils, though they prefer a rich, deep, friable loam. If it is naturally calcareous, so much the better. Other soils can be limed to counteract any acidity present. The early peas will grow well in a light sandy soil, but the varieties that come later will appreciate a soil which retains moisture.

Manuring Peas are not in the ground long before they grow and start to crop, and so the period in which they have the opportunity for collecting plant food is brief. For this reason plant foods should be applied sufficiently early, so that they are in such a form that the roots can collect and absorb them rapidly.

Well-prepared compost should be used and this should be used at two bucketsful to the square yard. This only needs lightly forking in. Sedge peat can be worked into the top 2 ins in the case of sandy soils and may be damped well first. In addition to the compost, fish manure or meat and bone meal should be applied at 4 oz per square yard. Potash should be given in addition in the form of wood ashes at 5 oz to the square yard.

Preparation of Soil Much has been said already about the preparation of the soil in the paragraphs dealing with manuring. When the actual time of sowing comes, drills may be drawn out with a draw hoe, 3 ins deep.

Seed Sowing In these flat drills the seed should be sown as evenly spaced as possible. If the seeds can be 2 ins apart each way, the plants have a chance of growing properly. The later varieties can even do with 3 ins distances. Many people sow peas thicker than this in the hope of getting heavier crops. It is seldom, however, that thick sowing gives better results than spaced sowing. The seed should be soaked in a mixture of paraffin and red lead for a couple of hours. When making up this liquid, the consistency should be like cream. The rows may be protected when the plants are just coming through by using home-made or bought pea-guards.

The rows of peas may be spaced at different distances according to the height of the variety sown. A 3 ft variety will need 18 ins on either side of it, while a 4 ft variety should have 2 ft.

There are three main times for sowing : (a) the early crop (autumn sown); (b) the main crop; and (c) the autumn crop.

The Early Crop, Autumn Sown In the south and in the very sheltered parts of the north, most years it is possible to make a sowing of one of the round seeded varieties during the winter months. I have been successful from sowings made in November.

The soil where the seed is to be sown should be on the dry side. For this reason it is a good plan to draw out the drill in the morning on a warm day to let it dry out, and then to carry out the seed-sowing in the afternoon.

Such sowings should be protected from the cutting winds. It is usual, therefore, to erect dwarf screens for the purpose and to stick the rows early. Some years it is necessary to place straw along the rows before and during a frosty period.

Another sowing can be made at the beginning of February although in the north gardeners must wait until the end of March. The variety chosen should be a round-seeded one.

The Main Crop From the beginning of April onwards, peas may be sown at regular intervals. Most gardeners make a rule to make another sowing as soon as the last one is showing above ground. The wrinkled-seeded varieties, being more tender than the round-seeded ones, may be sown thicker in the rows.

The Autumn Crop The earliest varieties may be sown again late in June or the beginning of July, so as to get good pickings in the month of September. It is usually possible to make these sowings on land from which the potatoes or early cauliflowers have been harvested. When drawing the drills out at this time of the year, they should be given a good flooding, as they are likely to be dry.

General Cultivation From the time that the peas first come through, hoeing should be carried out on either side of the rows. In the rows themselves, hand weeding may have to be done in the early stages. In addition to the occasional hoeings, it may be necessary to water during dry years, as moisture is essential to the roots. Mulches may be given along the rows to help retain the moisture and powdery sedge peat is useful for this purpose. It is better, when watering, to do this in small drills on either side of the row rather than on the row itself.

To help the plants to climb, little bushy twigs should be inserted in the ground near the peas 3 or 4 ins high. Staking should be done, except for the dwarfer types. The sticks may be placed 6 ins away from the row and 1 ft apart, and light, bushy sticks should be used. They should be perpendicular so the air can circulate and the peas do not tend to push through, as they do if the sticks slant inwards. Where sticks are not available nylon netting on special plastic posts may be used.

During the first hoeings, the earth should be brought up to the rows and not away from them. A kind of earthing-up operation is done as soon as plants are 3 or 4 ins high. This earthing-up helps to keep the plants upright.

Harvesting Peas should be picked regularly and no pod should be missed, when ready. When a few pods are left on a plant to go to seed, the cropping power of the plant is immediately reduced. Systematic picking ensures heavier crops.

Varieties There are two main groups : (a) The Round and (b) The Wrinkled. Marrowfat peas, which have such a delicious flavour, are Wrinkled Varieties and contain more sugar. However, the Round peas are hardier.

Earlies mature in 12 weeks. Second Earlies mature in 14 weeks. Main crops mature in 15 or 16 weeks. Late varieties take 17 weeks.

Early Varieties Dwarf Round-Seeded : *Meteor*. Very dwarf

but very hardy. Can be sown any time from September in one year to June the next. Only grows 1 ft high. *Early Bird.* A very popular variety for sowing in the north. Heavy Cropper. Dwarf Wrinkled Seeded : *English Wonder.* A dwarf marrowfat, much liked in the west, 18 ins. *Kelvedon Wonder.* Perhaps the best of the dwarf marrowfat, 18 ins. Grand for small gardens and allotments. *Little Marvel.* Best flavoured marrowfat, quick grower, 8 peas to a pod; may be ready in 11 weeks; 18 ins.

Tall Early : *Springtide.* A very heavy cropper, 3 ft, one of the earliest talls known. *Foremost.* Very heavy cropper, may be sown end of February in south for gathering end of May, 2½ ft. *Recette.* 2½ ft, wrinkle seeded type, triple podded. Well filled pods, very delicious.

Early Maincrops : *The Lincoln.* One of my favourites; grows only 2 ft high but crops very heavily. Marrowfat. *Kelvedon Spitfire.* 2½ ft. Plants smothered with pairs of deep green plump pods containing 8 or 9 plump peas each.

Maincrops : *Onward.* Perhaps the most popular pea of all, 2½ ft; produces dark green stumpy pods with peas of a high quality; said to be the most resistant variety to mildew; first-class flavour; marrowfat. *Green Shaft.* A variety resistant to disease, 2½ ft; large-podded, heavy cropper; well worth growing. *Lord Chancellor.* An excellent table variety, crops heavily, 3 ft; long, straight pods. *Histon Kingsize.* A vigorous very late variety, crops heavily, height 3–4 ft; excellent for the Show Bench. *Gladstone.* A good variety for drought areas; excellent Exhibition pea, 4 ft; pods pointed, curved; peas of good flavour. *Histon Maincrop.* Dark green medium-sized pods, 2½ ft; immense crop.

Potato

The potato is one of the most important crops in the garden, not only because in this country, at the present time, we eat more potatoes than any other vegetable, but also because it acts as a cleaning crop.

Soil Potatoes can be grown on all soils, though some produce those of an inferior flavour to others. It is said that the heavy clays and the peaty soils produce 'waxy' tubers. The ideal soil would be a deep, well-drained medium soil not a pure clay or too light a sand. Potatoes should not be grown under trees, or where the atmosphere is likely to be stagnant, for under such conditions the foliage is soft, and as a result potato blight will ravage the crop.

Preparation of Soil One of the best ways of preparing the soil for potatoes is by covering it liberally with rather rough compost. The alternative is to use partly rotted straw. This is done in the autumn. The rows should run due north to south, so that the sun can fall equally on either side of these.

Manuring The land should be manured in the autumn but more compost may be applied in the rows in the spring at planting time. Compost is applied at the rate of about one good barrow-load to 10 square yards.

The following should be applied along the rows : a fish manure at 3 oz per yard run or another organic fertilizer like meat and bone meal.

In the case of the very early potatoes, there is no need to give organic artificials in addition, as the potatoes are out of the ground before they can make use of the extra plant food.

Purchasing the Seed The main thing is to get tubers from plants free from virus diseases. With every pound of 'seed' purchased the grower should obtain the certificate number. This is his guarantee.

The tubers used for seed should be about the size of a hen's egg and weigh about $2\frac{1}{2}$ oz. Those who obtain larger tubers should cut these in such a way that each half contains the necessary eyes. Thus cutting should take place just before the tubers are planted.

Boxing Directly the potatoes are bought they should be boxed up, and placed in shallow trays to sprout rose end upwards. The rose end is the end where most of the eyes are found, and is the opposite end to that which was attached to the underground stem.

The farmer uses a potato tray $2\frac{1}{2}$ ft long, $1\frac{1}{2}$ ft wide, and $3\frac{1}{2}$ ins deep. In the corners there are small square posts standing 3 ins above the sides. These posts are there so that the trays may be stood one above the other while the sprouting process is going on, without injuring the sprouts.

The trays containing the potatoes should then be stacked in a cool, light, airy place where there is no possibility of their being frozen. When the tubers start to grow, some disbudding may take place, but be sure to leave the two strongest shoots at the rose end of the tuber. When the time comes for planting, the trays should be taken out into the garden and placed on top of the furrows. The sets should then be taken out one at a time and placed carefully in the bottom of the furrows without breaking off the sprouts. If planting is done carelessly, the sprouts will break off easily and all the trouble spent on them in the trays will be useless.

The object of sprouting the seed is to secure a few weeks' growth before planting takes place. Sprouted potatoes are ready to lift several weeks earlier than potatoes planted unsprouted. This saving of time also ensures heavy crops, as potatoes have, in consequence, a longer season of growth.

Planting   The earliest potatoes may be planted in shallow V-shaped drills 18 ins apart, and the tubers placed 1 ft apart in the rows. When planted in this way the tubers should be dug up when they are quite small.

Ordinary early potatoes will be 1 ft 9 ins apart, and the tubers 1 ft apart in the rows. The second earlies may be in in ridges 2 ft 3 ins apart, and the seed placed 1 ft 3 ins apart in the rows, while the latest varieties may be planted 2 ft 6 ins by 1 ft 6 ins. It is quite easy to enlarge the distances should the potatoes be particularly heavy croppers, or the soil exceedingly good.

The potatoes should not be planted deeper than 3 ins, and in the case of the earlier varieties a 2 in depth is sufficient. The rows will, of course, run north to south, and after the potatoes are in position, the compost, or rotten straw, may be drawn over them, leaving a very slight ridge. Planting will take place in the south round about the middle of March, and in the north during the second week in April.

On the whole, it is better to plant the late potatoes first and the early varieties last. In this way the late potatoes have a long season of growth and are not through the ground sufficiently quickly to be affected by a late spring frost. The early potatoes, on the other hand, being early maturers, give sufficiently heavy crops and yet, being planted later than the main crop varieties, probably miss the spring frosts.

General Cultivation   Directly the foliage appears through the ground the rows should be hoed. If there is any fear of frost, the compost may be drawn up to the plant, then, when the frosty period is over, this may be drawn back again.

When the tops are about half grown another slight

Planting potatoes shallowly in compost

earthing-up may be carried out on either side. This usually takes place when the stems above ground are 8 ins high. The ridges, however, should never be brought up too steeply, as if this is done the tubers may be exposed at the side.

During the growing period a sharp outlook should be kept for the potato blight, and directly, if not before, the disease is seen the leaves and stems should be given a thorough spraying with Bordeaux Mixture.

Harvesting   The rows of early potatoes may be lifted as soon as the tubers are of a suitable size. If the lifting can be done on a fine day, the tubers will come out clean and bright, and they look far more attractive in consequence.

The main crop need not be lifted to be stored until the haulm has died down. It is at this time that the tubers will be at their largest size and are certain to have firm skins.

It is a good plan to cut the haulm off the potatoes before digging up the tubers, especially if they have been attacked by potato blight, so no spores can drop on them and infest them.

The storing of the main crop may be done in a shed or cellar providing it is frost proof and dark. Potatoes, however, are often stored in clamps, or 'buries'. The ground on which these are to stand should be, if possible slightly higher than the general level of the soil, so that the tubers may be kept dry.

The potatoes are stacked in a long ridge-shaped heap 3 or 4 ft wide at the base and 2 or 3 ft high, and this triangular shaped mound is then covered with straw 6 ins deep. On top of the straw is put a 6 in covering of soil

Digging up potatoes, taking care not to injure them and (right) making a twist of straw at the top of the clamp for aeration.

taken from the ground surrounding the clamp. It is during this earthing operation that a trench may be made all round the clamp so as to carry away water. Ventilating holes should be given by means of a tuft of straw being allowed to project through the soil. If this is twisted hard, it will prevent the rain from percolating into the clamp. Ventilators are needed for every 6 ft length of clamp.

Varieties Earlies: *Ninety-Fold*. Probably the earliest potato of all, but apt to be soapy. *Epicure*. White round floury potato with good flavour. Attractive appearance. *Duke of York*. Bears kidney-shaped tubers. A firm yellow-fleshed variety. Non-immune. *Arran Pilot*. Ready 14 weeks from date of planting. Very heavy cropper, especially in the south. A good light land variety. Can be left in the ground as a second early without secondary growth taking place. Immune. *Arran Crest*. Very early. Heavy cropper, delicious potato. Immune.

Second Earlies: *Arran Banner*. A fine early main crop potato. Immune. A very heavy cropper. The tubers are white, round, and flattened. The flesh is white and the haulm tall and vigorous. *Arran Comrade*. A round variety, popular for exhibition purposes. The skin and flesh are white. Immune. *Eclipse*. A heavy cropping white-fleshed kidney. *Dr McIntosh*. Kidney, white fleshed, good cropper. *Maris Piper*. White-fleshed kidney. May become the best second early ever produced. Crops heavily. Immune to 'A' type eelworm. *Maris Peer*. Very heavy cropper, good quality, oval, white-fleshed. Should be eaten in August but will last in the ground until November. Resistant to Scab and Blight.

Main Crop: *Majestic*. An immune variety, being a heavy cropping white kidney. The tubers are generally large. *King Edward VII*. Probably the most popular kidney variety grown, the skin being pure yellow flushed with pink. An excellent cooker. A light cropper. Non-immune. *Arran Chief*. Bears a white round tuber. A heavy cropper. *Golden Wonder*. White-fleshed kidney. Immune. Excellent cooker. *Kerr's Pink*. Pink skinned – but white flesh. Heavy cropper, strong grower. *Pentland Dell*. Oval, white flesh – heavy cropper – good-sized tubers. *Pentland Crown*. Resistant to virus – heavy cropper – good storer and keeper. Good for Show.

Radish

Most people grow a few radishes even though they have quite a small garden. The old idea that the radish was hot, and so brought about indigestion, does not hold good today, as the introduction of new varieties, with their great improvements in flavour and form, has done much to increase the popularity of this vegetable.

Soil Radishes do not need deep soil, and they will grow equally well on heavy clays and sands for the summer, providing these are properly prepared. The main thing is that the soil should not be left lumpy and that the situation should not be such that the growth cannot be immediate and quick.

Preparation of Soil Little need be done except to see that the soil is in fine condition. In the case of light sands, the surface soil may be improved by forking in some organic matter such as fine peat or finely divided leaf mould.

Manuring Radishes are seldom given special manures though in all probability 2 oz of meat meal and 6 oz of wood ashes forked into the top 2 or 3 ins would improve hungry land. Sedge peat, if damped first, is excellent for dry soils if forked in to the top 1 or 2 ins at ½ lb to the square yard.

Seed Sowing The great mistake beginners make is to sow radish seed too thickly. Broadcasting is usual, but, as this is difficult to do thinly, it is generally better to sow the seed in rows 6 ins apart and only ½ in deep. The soil should always be made firm after sowing.

Cloches Good crops of radishes may be obtained at almost any time of the year from sowings made under cloches, or Access frames. However, plenty of organic matter must be worked into the soil first.

Outdoor Sowings It is possible to sow radishes outside in December in a special sheltered, sunny place. The bed should be raised, so as to be certain that the drainage is perfect, and the seed is broadcast on to the bed and raked in. Immediately afterwards the bed should be covered with straw to a depth of 4 ins. When the seed has germinated, the straw may be raked off so as to allow the plants to grow in the light.

When there is any sign of frost or snow, the straw should be replaced to give protection, and as soon as possible when the weather gets warmer the straw may be removed altogether.

These beds should be no wider than 4 ft, so that all the straw-moving, thinning, and other operations can be done without treading on the beds.

The next sowing may be made in a warm, dry border in February, and this can be covered with litter as before. These winter sowings are more possible in the south than the north, and succeed better on the eastern side of England, where the rainfall is lower.

Further sowings may be made from, say, the middle of March to the beginning of September, and these summer sowings prefer a cool, shady position. A north border of the garden is often convenient for this purpose.

In all cases the rows should be 6 ins apart, and the radishes thinned and pulled early.

Radishes may always be regarded as an intercrop, and can often be sown between seed-beds, between rows of other vegetables like peas, beans or carrots. They may be sown in the rows of vegetables, like asparagus, parsnips, and seakale, whose seeds take a long time to germinate, as the radishes then mark out the rows and provide an intercrop as well.

Radishes for the Winter It is possible to sow what are known as winter radishes during the month of July in the north and in August in the south in drills 9 ins apart, and, when the plants grow, to thin them out to 6 ins in the rows. These radishes are more like turnips, and can either be used in salads or are boiled and used as a cooked vegetable. The roots may be left in the ground and dug up as desired.

General Cultivation Constant hoeing in between the rows is necessary. Dustings with Derris and Pyrethrum dust to keep down the flea beetle has to be done most years, while occasional waterings during dry periods will help keep the radishes from going to seed.

Harvesting The radishes must be pulled regularly while they are fresh and young.

Varieties Round : *Red Turnip.* Bright colour. Crisp and tender. *Scarlet Globe.* Delicious flavour. Good size and tender. *Cherry Belle.* Bright scarlet in colour, crisp flesh, slow to go pithy.

Oval : *French Breakfast.* Deep crimson colour, with white flesh inside. Has small leaves, the root being solid and sweet. *French Breakfast, Early Forcing.* An excellent variety for a frame. Ready much earlier than the French Breakfast.

Long : *Icicle.* A handsome crisp white variety of good shape and quality.

Winter : *Black Spanish Long.* Has black skin, but firm white flesh. *China Rose.* A round pink variety.

Savoy Cabbage

The Savoy may be regarded as the winter cabbage, as it will stand, and in fact is improved by, frost. The cabbage has smooth leaves while the savoy has dark, deeply crinkled leaves.

Soil On the whole, this crop grows best on heavy, deeply cultivated rich land. If during cultivation the ground can be firmed, better hearted crops result. The Savoy does well following a crop like early potatoes or early peas.

Preparation of Soil As it is definitely related to the Brussels sprout, the conditions which suit this crop will suit the Savoy.

Manuring If the Savoys are to follow a previous crop, it is *possible,* directly this has been cleared, to sow fish manure on the surface of the ground at 4 oz to the square yard. This should be done in fact about a fortnight before the plants are put out.

Seed Sowing Seed may be sown in three batches, the first during the middle of March on a well prepared, warm seed-bed. A second sowing may be made at the beginning of April, and another sowing at the end of April.

The seeds should be sown in drills 18 ins apart, and directly the seedlings appear they may be thinned to 2 or 3 ins apart, and the thinnings transplanted into further seed-beds 6 ins square if desired. The rows should be kept free from weeds.

Planting Out The plants may be put out into their permanent position towards the end of June and during the month of July. If this is done on showery days, they will grow quickly, and if the weather is dry it would be better to puddle them in. The rows should be, in the case of the smaller varieties, 17 ins between the rows, and 15 ins in the rows, while the strong-growing varieties need planting 2 ft square.

General Cultivation There is nothing to be done except to hoe between the rows when necessary and to remove the stalk directly the Savoy has been cut.

Varieties Small Types : *Dwarf Green Curled.* A beautiful curled deeply coloured Savoy. Is very hardy, and of delicious flavour.

Early : Sow March. Cut September–October. *Best of All.*
Drumhead which forms firm, solid hearts generally late in
October. *Improved Early Drumhead.* Similar to above but
with firmer heart on the whole.

Mid-Season : Sow early April, cut November–February.
Savoy King. Light green soled – good flavour.

Late : Sow end of April, cut January–March. *Irish Giant
Drumhead.* Typical drumhead type, firm, delicious. Stands
until April. *Latest of All.* Bears intensely curled leaves.
Dark green, delicious.

Extra Late : Sow end April, cut following March. *Omega.*
Slow grower. Well worth waiting for. *Ormskirk Late
Green.* Will withstand very severe weather. Cuts from
January to the end of March.

Seakale

Seakale is not one of the commonest of vegetables, and yet
when grown it is much liked.

Soil The seakale seems to grow best on a heavy soil,
though it will grow well on an easily worked sandy loam.
Those who intend to lift the roots for forcing them under
cover will prefer such a soil, as it makes root-lifting easier.
The soil should be well-drained, and the situation should
be open and free from shade.

Preparation of Soil In March the soil may be levelled
by forking it over ready for planting. During the forking
over of the soil, powdery compost should be added.

Manuring This should be used at the rate of one good
barrowload per 10 square yards.

Also, use a fertilizer like fish manure, dried poultry
manure, meat and bone meal etc at 4 oz to the square yard
plus wood ashes at 4 oz to the square yard. In the spring,
after growth has commenced, dried blood may be applied
at about 2 oz to the yard run. Seakale appreciates a manuring with old seaweed. This for those who live by the sea !

Propagation Seakale may be propagated in two ways :
either by sowing seed or by means of root cuttings or
thongs. It takes two years to produce forcing crowns from
seed, though the plants thus raised are generally more
vigorous. Thongs are usually used.

When seed-sowing is practised, it is done in a fine seedbed in drills 12 ins apart and 1 in deep. The seedlings are
thinned out when they are 2 ins high to 6 ins apart. The
following February the plants are dug up, and are planted

out into their permanent positions. Just before planting, the top may be cut off just below the crown, as this makes flowering less likely.

Thongs are prepared from the clean, straight side-roots which grow out from the main root. The best of these side-roots are selected, of the thickness of a lead pencil or thicker. They are then cut into pieces 6 ins long, the thickest end of the thong being cut level and the thinner end cut slanting. By this means the gardener knows which is the top of the thongs, in spring, and can plant them the right way up.

After preparation, the thongs may be tied into bundles and put in layers of damp sand. They can remain covered with sand until planting-time comes round, and when uncovered it will be found that the top end of the roots have made several eyes. All these, except the two strongest should be rubbed off.

Planting Planting may take place during the third week in March, the thongs being put out in rows 18 ins apart and 15 ins apart in the rows. The top of the thong should be 1 in below the surface of the soil. Planting must be done firmly.

General Cultivation Throughout the summer, hoe when necessary between the rows. Any flowering stems that appear should be removed. By the middle of October, if the foliage has not already died, it should be cut off.

Forcing In the winter, when the foliage has died, the roots may be dug up and taken under cover to be forced, the side-roots being removed to form thongs for the following year. They can be forced under the staging of glasshouses, or in cellars. They should be stood upright in soil or rotted leaves and moisture may be given by regular sprayings with tepid water. The roots should be kept in the dark. The temperature should be no higher than 60°F.

It is also possible to force growing in the open, by covering the crowns with a forcing-pot or box and then surrounding it with farmyard manure. This may be put on the beds to the depth of 6 ins, and will create sufficient heat to cause the seakale to grow. In the course of three weeks or so the well-blanched heads should be ready for cutting.

Those who intend to force the roots outside will do well to plant the thongs in such a way that three crowns may be covered by one forcing-pot. This means planting them on the triangular system.

'Natural' seakale is also liked. In this case the rows are usually 15 ins apart, and the rows may be raked clean in the autumn and then earthed up to a depth of 8 ins or so. This earthing-up should be done during a fine period and not when the soil is wet and sodden. The seakale will then grow through the earthed-up portion, and when the tops of the shoots are seen through the ridge – cutting may begin. This may be done by means of a sharp spade, the heads should be cut $\frac{1}{2}$ in below the crown.

When all the crowns have been cut, the soil may be thrown down and the cut stems covered with 1 in. of soil.

The rows should be well manured with compost every year. Apply it at a bucketful a yard run. It should be possible to grow natural seakale in this way without disturbing the rows, for six years.

Shallot

The shallot is one of the easiest vegetables to grow, and is used for pickling purposes.

SOIL It grows well on any soil, though it prefers a light loam, deeply worked and well drained.

Preparation of Soil The soil may be prepared as for onions.

Planting The bulbs are planted as early as possible, the old rule being to plant on the shortest day so as to harvest on the longest day of the year. In the south it is possible to plant in January or early February, though in the north it is necessary to delay until well on in March. The rows should be 12 ins apart and the bulbs spaced out, according to the variety, 4 to 6 ins apart in the rows.

Planting may be done in all kinds of 'odd' places – along the tops of celery trenches, as an edging to the garden, or on land that is to be used subsequently for other crops.

Before planting, the soil should be firmed so that the bulbs may be pushed in to half their depth. Any loose skins or dead tops should be removed, for worms have a "nasty" habit of trying to draw these parts down into the soil and thus may pull the bulbs out. Firm planting is necessary.

A fortnight after planting, the bed should be examined and any bulbs that are loose should be firmed and those that have been removed may be replaced.

General Cultivation The rows should be hoed when necessary, but not deeply, taking care neither to cut the bulbs nor to bury them, as the shallot prefers to grow on the surface of the soil.

Harvesting In July the leaves of the shallot will be seen to be turning yellow, and by the second or third week the bulbs may be lifted and left on the surface of the soil to complete the drying off. After a few days they may be placed on a path or a concrete yard and turned over two or three times, to make certain that they are thoroughly dry. After this they may be divided and stored in a cool, dry place.

Varieties *The Russian Shallot.* Sometimes called the Dutch or Jersey shallot. Throws a larger and rounder bulb than the true variety. The skin is of a coppery-red colour. *The True Red or Yellow Shallot.* May be obtained in these two colours. It throws a nice firm bulb of the right size for pickling.

Spinach

Various kinds of spinach are grown for the table. These are the summer spinach, the winter spinach, the spinach beet or perpetual spinach, and the New Zealand spinach. *The Annual Spinach : Summer and Winter.* Both the summer and winter spinach may be classed as annuals.

Soil A shallowly tilled loam produces first class spinach, and good crops may even be obtained on heavy clay. Spinach tends to go to seed quickly on very light soils, and, to prevent this, such soils should be enriched with plenty of moisture-holding material, like sedge peat or compost.

Manuring When preparing the soil as much compost as possible should be incorporated so as to give the spinach the moisture-holding material it appreciates. In order to encourage quick growth, liquid manure may be given along the rows, at fortnightly intervals, directly the plants have started into growth.

Sowing the Seed The summer spinach should be sown towards the beginning of March in a warm, sheltered position. Two or three sowings may be made from this date onwards at ten-day intervals. As the weather gets warmer the sowings should be made in the moister situations, and to ensure immediate germination the seed should be soaked in water for twenty-four hours.

The drills should be made 1 ft apart and 1 in deep, and directly the seedlings can be handled they should be thinned out to 6 ins apart along the rows. Few people realize the importance of thinning spinach, but, like most other vegetables, it appreciates room for development.

The winter spinach may be sown from the first week in August to the middle of September at intervals of a fortnight. It is often necessary with these conditions to make special raised beds, 5 ft wide, 2 or 3 ins above the level of the soil around. In this way the rain can get away quickly in the alleyways, and, because of the comparatively narrow width of the beds, the crop can be gathered without treading on the soil.

The rows under this system may be 9 ins apart, and when the plants are through the seedlings may be thinned to 4 ins apart.

General Cultivation The rows must be hoed when necessary and if possible mulched during the summer with fine compost or sedge peat. The winter spinach may need protection, and this can be done by using straw over and between the rows. Bracken or heather may take the place of straw where they are easier to obtain. In the north it may be necessary during a frosty period to cover the rows with continuous cloches or lights.

Harvesting Summer spinach should be picked regularly, and quite hard. It does not matter if you remove the majority of leaves from the plant.

The winter spinach should not be picked hard or the plants will be spoilt. The largest leaves should be taken, and they should be gathered singly. Only a moderate proportion of leaves should be removed from each plant.

Varieties Summer: *Improved Round Victoria*. A round seeded variety; it is very long-standing and bears medium green leaves. *Monarch Long Standing*. One of the broadest-leaved round-seeded spinach grown.

Winter: *New Giant Leaved*. A prickly-seeded variety, large leaved and very long standing. May be sown in the spring as well as in August. *Long Standing New Prickly*. Usually grown for winter and spring use. Is a hardy and abundant cropper.

Spinach Beet

Spinach Beet, sometimes called the perpetual spinach, is useful, as it produces a continues supply of large succulent leaves during hot summers. The leaves, being similar to the ordinary annual spinach, are sometimes a more popular substitute than New Zealand spinach.

Soil See Beetroot.

Manuring See Beetroot.

Seed Sowing The seed may be sown in April and a further sowing may be made at the beginning of August. In this way succession and regular cropping is obtained. The rows should be 15 ins apart and the plants should be thinned out to 8 ins apart.

General Cultivation Regular weeding, hoeing and occasional waterings are all that are necessary to keep the plants growing and cropping satisfactorily.

Harvesting The leaves must be gathered regularly directly they are large enough and even if they are not required. If this is not done, the older leaves will start to get coarse, and it should be the gardener's aim to keep up the supply of fresh leaves that are young and tender. It is usual to pick the leaf, stem and all, so as to ensure further leaves growing.

Seakale Spinach

This vegetable is listed as Seakale Spinach, though it is sometimes called the Swiss Chard. The main difference between this and the ordinary spinach is that the leaves are very large, thick, and silvery-white in colour. The stalks are served as seakale and the leaf part is dressed as spinach.

It is grown in exactly the same way as spinach beet, and should be harvested in the same way also. It is most important to pick both the stems and the leaves at the same time.

The delicious ivory-white stems of seakale spinach. The leaf part is eaten as spinach, the stem as seakale.

New Zealand Spinach

New Zealand spinach is not liked so much as ordinary spinach by some people, though when it is served on the table, properly sieved, few people can distinguish the difference in its flavour.

Soil This spinach grows quite well on the light dry soils and does not go to seed like the ordinary types. As it grows somewhat flat upon the ground, rather like ivy, it creates its own mulch. It will grow quite well on the heavier soils, providing they are well prepared.

Manuring See ordinary spinach.

Propagation The plants should be raised under glass by sowing seeds in a light compost in boxes round about the end of March. When the young seedlings come through they may be potted up singly into 3 in pots and set near the glass on a shelf, where they may grow until they are put out at the end of May.

Those who have frames handy may raise the seedlings by sowing two or three seeds in a 3 in pot during the second week of April, and, when the plants germinate, thinning them down to one if necessary. Those who have neither greenhouse nor frames may sow 'in situ' under continuous cloches about the third week of March, or the seed can be sown out of doors about the second week of May.

Planting Out The plants should be put out in rows 3 ft apart, the plants being 2 ft apart in the rows. This space will soon be covered, and the plants may become interlaced if they are not cut back and picked regularly.

General Cultivation The plants should never be allowed to become overcrowded, and so the end growths may be pinched back from time to time, these tops being particularly delicious. The 'stopping' will cause further branching to take place, and a prolific little bush will thus be formed.

Regular hoeing may be necessary, until the plants cover the ground. Though it has been suggested – and it is perfectly true – that this spinach will grow in dry soil where ordinary varieties go to seed, there is no reason to suppose that the plants will not grow all the better for copious waterings during the dry seasons.

Swede

Swedes are often preferred to winter turnips. Swedes have a delicacy flavour of quite a different character from turnips, and when grown for household use garden varieties should be chosen.

Manuring See Turnips.

Seed Sowing The seed may be sown in drills 18 ins apart, the plants being thinned out to 1 ft apart, as in the case of winter turnips. Seed in late May or early June.

General Cultivation See Turnips.

Harvesting Swedes are usually left outside throughout the winter, and may be drawn as desired. It is seldom that they are seriously damaged by frost.

Varieties *Purple Top Swede.* Clean, well-shaped roots of good colour and flavour. *Bronze Top Swede.* Similar to above, except that the foliage is of a different colour. It is said by epicures to be the better flavoured.

Tomato

It is possible to grow tomatoes out of doors, and in good summers heavy crops can be obtained in the open. During wet autumns it is difficult to ripen tomatoes outside, and they are then usually attacked by the potato blight.

Soil Tomatoes may be grown on both heavy and light soils providing they are well drained.

Preparation of Soil The heavy soils should have a heavy top dressing of compost or sedge peat given.

Manuring Well-made compost should be forked in lightly at one good barrowload to 10 square yards, and, in addition, a 'complete' fish manure or other organic fertilizer should be used at 4-5 oz to the square yard.

During dry seasons it may be necessary to add a little more 'food', and this may be applied in the form of Seaweed liquid manure at half a gallon to the square yard in July. During wet seasons, however, wood ashes may be given and two applications may be necessary at, say, 4 oz to the square yard.

Liquid Feeding To feed tomatoes use seaweed liquid manure or liquid farmura. This can be applied after each truss has set or if preferred as a regular routine every 7 days after the first fruits have appeared. This can be obtained in bottles and is organic in its base. This makes it possible to apply exactly the right quantities of 'balanced' food wherever desired.

Seed Sowing The seed may be sown under glass, during the middle of March, either in boxes, or in pots. Boxes are on the whole preferable as in this way numbers of seedlings can conveniently be moved when potting-up time comes.

Tomato seeds should be spaced evenly all over the box $\frac{1}{4}$ in apart, and be pushed in with the point of a pencil $\frac{1}{4}$ in deep into the soil. The boxes should be covered with a piece of glass, and over this a sheet of brown paper should be placed. The boxes should then be placed in a frame over the hot-bed, or in a greenhouse at a temperature of about 55°F. In the frame the boxes should be within 6 ins of the glass.

Directly the seedlings grow, the glass and the brown paper are removed, and in the greenhouse they should be placed on a shelf near the light. Watering must be done carefully, and water at the same temperature as the house or frame should be given through a fine rose. The tomato soil should never be over-wet. Water should be given just

This excellent outdoor variety known as Outdoor Girl crops heavily and produces delicious tomatoes.

Start of the very early tomatoes, the little plants growing in their boxes like regimented soldiers. This is because the seeds have been sown exactly 1 in square.

before the boxes are covered or recovered with a sheet of glass.

Transplanting   About the end of March or beginning of April the plants should have grown well, and they may then be transplanted 2 ins apart into other boxes, or be potted-up singly into 3 in pots. The compost should be similar.

At this stage the plants should be handled tenderly and the stems should not be pinched with the thumb and forefinger, as otherwise they will damp off. It is easier to handle them by the leaves. When potting, they should be made firm and watered in.

The boxes or pots can then be put back into the frames or on to the greenhouse shelf again. The frames should be shut down and shaded for a few days until the plants get used to their new conditions. After this, ventilation can be given, and the lights removed altogether on the warm, bright days. In the house, ventilation should be given whenever possible, so as to get the plants growing sturdily. If they tend to get long and lanky, the slightest sprinkling of wood ashes will often tone down the growth.

Towards the end of April or beginning of May the plants in the greenhouses should be hardened off by placing them into frames and by giving them plenty of room also. Those in frames may then be stood outside with some protection.

Planting Out It should be possible to put the tomatoes out, about the end of May or beginning of June. Those who do not want the bother of raising their own plants may buy plants from a nurseryman. The specimens that are bought should be sturdy and 'hard' and about 8 ins high. The gardener should never be hurried about planting out tomatoes, for it is better to wait a fortnight or so until the soil and the weather are suitable.

The plants that are still in boxes should be prepared for planting by passing a knife both ways in between the plants and cutting the roots right down to the bottom of the boxes. If a good watering is done after this, it will be found easy to lift out the plants with a square block of soil attached to the roots, with the result that planting can be carried out without any check to the young plants.

Tomatoes growing on the tripod or Tepee system, by which three plants are trained up bamboos to an apex.

The hole for planting should not be too deep, and the gardener's aim should be to bury the roots so that they are covered with $\frac{1}{2}$ in of new soil. Firm planting is necessary and in order to prevent the plants becoming damaged by the winds they should be supported at once by pushing a bamboo into the ground close by and tying the plant up 'loosely' to it.

Where a large number of plants are grown, two good posts can be put at the ends of the rows and wires stretched tightly between them. This enables the plants to be tied up to the wires where they grow. Where there are walls or fences, the tomatoes may be grown against these, and a sunny south border is most suitable for this.

General Cultivation Directly the plants are in, the land should be lightly hoed and this hoeing may be done occasionally throughout the season, unless the soil is completely mulched with sedge peat then hoeing is unnecessary.

Remove the side-shoots regularly. These seem to grow at a great pace. If they are removed whilst they are small, the best results are achieved. It is possible to grow these plants on one or two main stems.

As new growth takes place, so must tying be attended to, and thick, green cotton twine is very satisfactory for this purpose. When tying, a space should always be left for the stem to swell.

During the first week of August it is advisable to stop the plants – that is, to pinch off the end of the main stem and so permit no further growth. More side-shoots will then push out as a result but these must be removed as they appear.

It is unwise to allow the leaves to form a dense mass which excludes the sunlight and air, but, on the other hand, the leaves manufacture plant foods which feed the fruits. Those plants which have plenty of room to grow may be allowed to retain all their leaves. When planting closer, whole leaves may be removed here and there, right back to the main stem. It is better to do this than to cut back a large number of the leaves by half. The leaves as they turn yellow and become useless should be cut off.

It may be necessary to spray tomatoes as a preventive against potato blight. A Bordeaux mixture is used for this purpose.

Harvesting The fruit should be picked as it ripens, and

A dwarf tomato, Histon Cropper

very often it has to be gathered just as it is turning red if blackbirds and thrushes are taking their toll. It is fairly easy to continue the ripening of the fruit indoors if it is placed in warmth.

At the end of September all the fruits should be removed and ripened by hanging the trusses over a wire indoors. The fruit may be kept, if desired, in a deep box of bran (rather in the way that children's presents are placed in a bran tub), and they will keep in this way for a long time and ripen off satisfactorily.

Varieties *Golden Amateur.* Dwarf, golden variety. *Sioux.* Medium-sized fruit, good quality and flavour. *Amateur Improved.* Dwarf variety – crops heavily – smallish tomatoes. *Histon Cropper.* Compact plant – medium-sized fruit. Resistant to blight. *Easicrop.* Dwarf, blood red fruit, firm and fleshy, excellent for sandwiches. *Outdoor Girl.* A heavy cropper of good quality. *Growers Pride.* Vigorous early – resistant to disease – can be grown in the open.

Turnip

A turnip is more than a large, rather hard root which is used in the winter and has to be mashed to make it palatable. There are many varieties which grow no bigger than a tennis ball, which are tender and delicious when cooked.

Turnips belong to the cabbage family, and so are liable to attacks by the same pests and diseases.

Soil A sandy loam is said to be the most suitable soil for turnips. On soils lacking in humus, plants have a tendency to run to seed, and, furthermore, they are usually very badly attacked by the Turnip Flea Beetle.

Manuring The lighter soils should be kept rich in organic matter which will help to retain the moisture. When grown as a main crop, turnips may be given the same feeding as advised for beetroot, but, in addition, lime should be applied on the surface of the soil at 4 oz to the square yard just before sowing the seed.

Seed Sowing *Early Outside*. It should be possible to sow turnips during the early part of March in a sheltered spot, providing the ground can be got down to a fine tilth. The rows in this case can be 8 ins apart and the seed sown evenly in the rows. When the seedlings are through they can be thinned out to 4 ins apart. In April another sowing may be made in drills 12 ins apart, the turnips being thinned to 6 ins apart when they are an inch or so high.
Main Crop. The main crop is generally sown in May, and in a shady position if possible. From such sowings it is possible to pull useful roots in the late summer.
Winter Turnips. In this case a sowing is made from the middle of July to the end of August. The drills should be 18 ins apart, the plants being thinned to 6 ins apart in the early stages, and to 1 ft apart when the roots are fit to use.

General Cultivation In the case of earlier sowings, it is of the utmost necessity to keep a sharp lookout for the Turnip Flea Beetle. Regular dustings with Derris dust should be done, even before the little plants are through the ground.

The soil must be hoed not only to kill weeds, but to conserve moisture needed by this crop. In very dry seasons it may be necessary to water. When watering is done a good sprinkler should be used for half an hour or more, and a mulching of sedge peat may be given immediately afterwards in order to help conserve the moisture.

Turnips
Red Top Milan, Snowball and Golden Ball

Harvesting The spring and summer-sown varieties should be pulled while they are young and fresh. In this way they are used before they get coarse.

The winter varieties may stand outside and be used as desired, though in the northern districts, which experience frosts, they should be lifted and clamped as for potatoes.

Varieties Early in Frame: *Sutton's Gem.* Delicious oval turnip quite different from any other variety. Those who haven't eaten this don't know what a turnip can be.

Early Outside and Main: *Tokyo Cross.* Globe-shaped pure white, very early. *Extra Early White Milan.* The roots are flat, of medium size, and quite smooth; the flesh is white and the flavour is much appreciated. *Selected Early Snowball.* A perfectly formed round white turnip with a short top and a single tap root; the flesh is white, solid and mild. *Early White Stone.* An early turnip; roots somewhat flat.

Winter Turnips: *Chirk Castle.* A good winter variety, firm white flesh. *Golden Ball.* A yellow-fleshed garden turnip; clean in growth.

7 Unusual Vegetables

There is now a quite considerable interest in the more unusual type of vegetable – due no doubt to the increasing popularity of holidays abroad. Tourists are served with such delicious novelties as capsicum and eggplants in foreign restaurants and hotels, and soon acquire a taste for them. I have grown all the following crops, and have had them all cooked for me at home.

Artichoke Chinese

Ivory white tubers are produced in abundance, and can be used from November to April, either cooked or in salads. They may be boiled, fried, or eaten raw. The plant only grows 18 ins high.

Propagation By means of the tubers produced the previous year.

Planting This is carried out in April, usually in drills 6 ins deep. The rows should be 18 ins apart and the tubers placed 9 ins apart in the rows. An open sunny situation should be chosen.

Soil The most suitable soil is a well-drained free-working loam. The tubers rot off in badly drained land. Light soils should be improved by the addition of humus in the form of rotted leaves or peat.

Harvesting In well-drained soils the tubers may be left in the ground until required. It is possible to lift them from October onwards. They can be stored in soil or sand. It is unwise to keep them in a dry place, as the tubers may shrivel. When lifting, all the 'roots' that have formed should be removed. The tubers must be kept covered to preserve their whiteness; if exposed to the light they turn a disagreeable yellow colour.

Beans

Two unusual runner beans must be mentioned in this chapter. *The Blue Coco*, which as its name suggests, bears blue pods, and the *Robin Bean* which bears red speckled pods. Both should be grown exactly as the runner bean.

Beet

The seakale beet – or seakale spinach, as it is erroneously called – is grown for the thick white stems it produces and for the large green leaves growing at the ends of these stems, which are delicious when used as substitute for spinach.

Soil All soils, from the very light to the very heavy, seem to suit this vegetable.

Preparation of Soil Requires heavy composting and waterings from time to time with liquid manure.

Seed Sowing Sow seeds late in April or early in May in drills 15 ins apart. Despite thin sowing it will be necessary to thin so as to space the plants out to 12 ins apart in the rows.

Harvesting Pull the leaves and stems regularly and do not cut. In this way further stems and leaves are produced. (NB Put a teaspoonful of lemon-juice into the water in which the stalks are boiling, so as to preserve the brilliant white colour.)

Capsicum

These fruits always attract by their brilliance of colour when exhibited at shows. They can be used for flavouring pickles, for putting into salads, and for cooking in various ways. They are 'hot'. The fruit may be likened to a long queerly-shaped tomato, red and green.

Propagation Seeds should be sown in No-Soil compost in pots early in March, either in a glasshouse or in a heated frame. Place three seeds in a 3-in pot, and when the plants are growing keep the best plant and remove the other two. In late May they may be planted outside. In the north it will be probably be necessary to continue growing them in frames or under glass.

Planting If they can be planted out late in May or early in June the rows should be 18 ins apart, and the plants 18 ins apart in the rows. Outside they produce much finer and heavier crops, and will go on fruiting if the first ripened fruits are gathered.

General Cultivation They should be damped overhead from time to time in the afternoon or early evening to keep down red spider, and hoed regularly.

Harvesting They are picked regularly as the fruits ripen, and the whole crop is gathered before the end of September, when frosts may be expected.

Cardoon

This vegetable resembles the globe artichoke when growing. It has a very delicious 'nutty' flavour, and may be used as a vegetable or in soups.

Propagation The seed may be sown in pots late in March or early in April. There is no need to give them a lot of heat. They may be raised quite well in a cold frame. Water sparingly until the seedlings have grown well. Sow three seeds in each pot and thin out later, as suggested for capsicum. Some growers sow the seed in the shallow trenches where the plants are to grow in April or May.

Planting Trenches are made in advance 4 ins deep, 6 ins wide, and 4 ft apart. Compost is put into the bottom of the trench to a 3 in thickness, and this is forked in. The plants are put out 18 ins apart in the trench. If sowings are made in the trenches, two or three seeds are placed at 18 in distances. Cover these lightly with soil. When they grow, the plants are thinned down to one at each station.

General Cultivation The trenches should be given plenty of water, and weak seaweed liquid manure may be given once a week or so from June onwards. Do not earth-up before October, tie up the stems loosely, and wrap the plants round with brown paper. Bring up the soil to the plants. A month after earthing-up the cardoons are ready for use.

Harvesting Lift as desired and use.

Varieties *Spanish Cardoon* This is a variety usually grown, as it has spineless leaves. The fault is that it easily runs to seed.

Celerica

One of my favourite vegetables. It grows like a turnip and tastes like the heart of celery. It is excellent when sliced in salads or when cooked. It is easy to grow, and the vegetable will keep six months after it is fully grown.

Propagation The plants should be raised in exactly the same way as celery plants, pricking the seedlings out when large enough. Plant them out in May or early June in rows 12 ins apart, and the plants 12 ins apart on flat ground.

General Cultivation Keep the rows hoed. Celeriac is a gross feeder, and will need liquid manure from the end of June onwards once a week. Fish manure at 3 ozs per yard run may be given at the beginning of September as the roots plump up during this month and October. All the side-growths are removed.

Harvesting A fortnight before the roots are to be lifted the soil should be hoed well up into the foliage, to cause the upper part of the root to become blanched. Celeriac should be dug up and stored in soil in a shed.

Varieties *Paris Ameliore.* A good white French variety which grows a large bulb. *Erfurt.* This variety produces a much smaller root, though it is of first-class quality.

Egg-Plant

Often called Aubergine. It is a delicious vegetable when cooked. It may be stuffed and baked, cut into slices and fried, or flavoured and boiled. I find it delicious when fried.

Seed Sowing Sow the seed in January or February in a warm greenhouse or in March in a frame. In the house the temperature should be about 60 degrees F. Two or three seeds may be sown in a 3in pot; reducing down to one plant is necessary later on. After a month or six weeks pot the plants up into 6in pots, and leave them to grow on in these until ready for planting outside.

Planting In the north it will be better to grow them on in the frame. In the south they may be planted out 2 ft square on the south border or near a sunny wall.

General Cultivation The plants should always be grown on a single leg or stem at the start, then when they are a foot high the growing point is pinched out to make them branch. Four to six fruits should be allowed to form, and after this the lateral growths must be stopped. The plants should be syringed under the leaves on warm days to keep down red spider. The rows should be mulched with sedge peat, spread over the ground an inch deep.

Varieties *Long Purple.* Throws a large fruit, round and purplish in colour. It is often of very fine quality. *Blanche Longue de la Chine.* A long white eggplant of a delicious flavour. Seems to contain more 'meat' than the other varieties.

Garlic

Planting It should be planted at the same time as shallots, in January or February. Plant the 'cloves' 2 ins beneath the surface of the soil. The cloves may be put in as close as 9 ins. apart.

Harvesting As for shallots.

Good King Henry

This is known to some people as Mercury, and is one of the easiest vegetables to grow.

Seed Sowing Seeds are sown where the plants are to grow, in April or May in rows 2 ft apart, and the plants thinned out to 18 ins apart. It is possible to divide old plants and to choose the best roots and plant them out where they are to grow. Seeds, too, may be sown in a seedbed and the seedlings planted out.

General Cultivation If this plant is grown on well manured land, and is treated well, it will crop heavily from

April to June. It produces shoots which should be cut in their young stages and tied up into bundles, when they resemble asparagus. If the stems are allowed to get old, the skin toughens quickly and then it is necessary to remove this before they can be cooked.

Squashes and Pumpkins

Squashes and pumpkins may be grown in the same way as ridge cucumbers and marrows. The plants occupy a good deal of space, and so plenty of room should be allowed.

Propagation The plants are raised under glass from seed sown in pots in April or May. Sow two seeds to each 3-in pot. Later remove the weakest. It is also possible to sow the seeds where the plants are intended to remain, under upturned jam jars.

Planting Out If any old fermenting material such as grass mowings can be placed in a mound in order to give the young plants a hot-bed, so much the better. This heating-up of the soil gets them growing quickly from the start.

Harvesting Squashes and pumpkins may be harvested directly they are sufficiently big. They are edible in all their stages. Some – like winter types – can be hung up for use in winter, and the clever housewife can find a dozen or more different ways of cooking them. The squashes which throw the smaller fruits are very useful to train up trellis and fences. They then take up little room, and can be allowed to crop heavily. Many of them are decorative.

NB When the growing shoots are pinched off, they may be used and cooked as spinach.

Varieties (a) Squashes: *Hubbard Squash.* Should not be eaten till September or October; will keep until February; perhaps the most useful winter variety. *Banana Squash.* Has the consistency of a banana; delicious flavour; will keep on into the winter if necessary. *Acorn Squash.* Small variety, good flavour. *Gold Nugget.* Excellent flavour, quite round, good keeper.

(b) Pumpkins: *Hundredweight.* Orange coloured, huge fruits; edible and good.

A beautiful specimen of a Hubbard Squash. This excellent winter vegetable can be grown 'on the flat' as well as up a pole or fence.

Kohlrabi

In Europe, kohlrabi is a popular vegetable. There are two types, the green and the purple, the green being the more tender of the two. It is similar in flavour to the turnip, but has that 'nutty' flavour that turnips have not.

Seed Sowing Seed may be sown at any time from the

second week in March to the middle of August. The rows should be 2 ft apart, and the seedlings thinned to 3 ins apart in the rows in the early stages, and finally to 6 ins apart. The young plants pulled at this final thinning should be in a fit condition to use as a vegetable.

General Cultivation When hoeing, pull the earth away from the plants. In every other way they are treated as for turnips.

Harvesting The plants may be left in the ground until required, and will usually withstand quite hard frosts. Do not grow the roots too large as they become coarse. In very cold climates they may be dug up and stored in the same way as other root crops.

Sweet Corn

Soil It will grow well on almost any type of soil, providing it is properly fed with compost.

Preparation of Soil It does well on land that has been well manured for a previous crop. On light or hungry land it will be necessary to add compost in the spring. In all cases it helps to work half a bucketful of damped sedge peat into the top 2 ins of soil, plus fish manure, meat and bone meal, or hoof and horn meal, at 3 to 4 ozs to the square yard.

Seed Sowing Sweet Corn is better not transplanted, sow the seed out of doors under cloches during the second week of April, or in the North at the end of April. If cloches are not available sow out of doors in May. Draw the drills $1\frac{1}{2}$ ins deep and space the seeds 12 ins apart. The rows should be 2 ft apart.

General Cultivation Always give sweet corn full sunshine and arrange to plant the crop in a 'block' and not in one or two long rows, as this gives a better chance of pollination. In dry weather water well and mulch with damped sedge peat.

Harvesting After fertilization the grains pass through a watery, then a milky, and on to a doughy stage. The cobs are ready for eating at the milky stage, this usually $3\frac{1}{2}$ weeks from the time of flowering. The 'silks' will then be brown and withered. To tell the right stage, part of the sheath of the cob should be pulled back and one of the grains pressed with the thumb nail. The contents should spurt out and have the consistency of clotted cream. Use sweet corn as soon as possible after picking.

Cooking Strip off the husks, put the cobs in boiling water and serve hot with a smear of butter or margarine. Pepper and salt to taste.

Varieties *Kelvedon Glory* (F1 Hybrid). The earliest and best, ready the third week of July. Cobs usually 7 ins long. *Golden Bantam.* Very hardy, medium-sized, bright yellow. *Prima* (F1 Hybrid). Two weeks earlier than Golden Bantam with larger cobs of excellent flavour.

Onion
Welsh

This is really a herbaceous perennial, and came originally from Siberia. It is very hardy. Resembles spring onions.

Propagation Seed may be sown in July or August in order to produce a supply in the spring. Young plants are obtained by the division of older plants, and each onion plant when put out will produce thirty or forty onion plants around it.

Onion Tree

This is sometimes known as the Egyptian onion. Stems are thrown up from the bulbs on which clusters of small bulbs are produced. These are excellent for pickling. There may be a dozen small onions on the tops of the stems when the plants are well grown.

Planting The bulbs formed on the stem may be saved and planted out in shallow drills early in April. The rows should be 18 ins apart and the bulbs 6 ins apart.

General Cultivation If well grown, the plants will need some support as the little onions begin to form. Keep the soil firm around them for the first three weeks or so after planting as the birds often pull them up by means of the loose skins.

Harvesting in the Autumn Fork up the plant and, when dried off, remove the onions at the base and on the stems.

Parsley Hamburg

Hamburg parsley grows very much like a parsnip, while the leaves resemble parsley.

Seed Sowing The land should be prepared as for carrots, the seed should be sown in March in drills 18 ins apart, and the plants finally thinned to half that distance in the rows.

General Cultivation Hoe from time to time to keep down weeds. Apply whizzed napthalene at 2 oz per yard run between the rows to keep down the carrot fly.

Harvesting The roots should be in season from November to the following April, though they may be harvested as early as September if they are required. It is better to lift in November and to store as for beetroot.

Peas asparagus

These are rather fascinating to grow, as they look more like a vetch than the ordinary pea. They do not climb, but grow about 18 ins high in a bushy form. They have beautiful dark-red blossoms. The pods should be picked while they are young and fresh, about 1 in long. The pod is cooked as picked, and the flavour is unique, something like a cross between an asparagus and pea flavour.

Seed Sowing The seeds are sown where the plants are to grow at the same time as ordinary main crop peas. They grow quite well in the south border. The rows should be 18 ins to 2 ft apart. The seed is small, and so the little drills need be no deeper than $\frac{1}{2}$in.

General Cultivation Push in a few twiggy sticks to keep the plants upright.

Harvesting Pick regularly, to prevent seeds from forming inside the pods.

Peas sugar

These, usually called *Mange-tout* in France, are quite different from the ordinary peas. The pods have no tough interior skin, and thus when preparing them for the table all that need be done is to top and tail and then boil. The whole of the pod is edible.

Seed Sowing Sow the seed in May in rows 4 ft apart. The Mange-tout peas often grow to a height of 6 ft and require staking.

Harvesting Pick the pods regularly. They are more delicious when the pods are fresh and young. If the pods are allowed to set, cropping ceases.

A row of Sugar Peas.

Salsify

Salsify has been described as the vegetable oyster and certainly is a most delicious root crop.

Soil Requires a rather light soil. The soil should not have been recently enriched with fresh compost as this causes the roots to become over-long.

Preparation of Soil Well rotted compost should be

applied at one bucketful to the square yard. A good fish manure should be used in addition at the rate of 3–4 ozs to the square yard. Cultivate these into the soil 2 ins deep.

Seed Sowing Sow the seed in April, with drills 12 ins apart and 1 in deep. Directly the seedlings are large enough to be handled they may be thinned out first of all to 4 ins apart and then finally 8 ins apart.

General Cultivation Hoeing in between the rows is necessary to keep down weeds. The same care should be taken when hoeing as advised in the case of beetroot.

Harvesting Use the roots first of all during the second or third week of October. Like parsnips they come to no harm when left in the ground until required. Like beetroot they bleed if they are damaged when being lifted. If necessary dig the crop up early and store the roots in sand either outside or in a shed.

Scorzonera

May be grown in exactly the same manner as salsify. It is quite different in appearance, the root is black and the leaves wider. Actually the two plants belong to different

Salsify, the most delicious root vegetable is sometimes called 'the vegetable oyster'.

families. The roots are often left in the ground a second year and then they are much larger.

Rhubarb

Rhubarb is used as a fruit from a culinary point of view, but it is usually grown in every vegetable garden and so is included in this book.

Seed Sowing Being a permanent crop the soil should be prepared as for Seakale. Plants may be raised from seed sown in March in drills 1 in deep and 1 ft apart, the seedlings being thinned to 10 ins. Plant out into their permanent positions when they are a year old, in rows 3 ft apart and 2½ ft between the plants.

Propagation The easier method of propagation is by division. Do this in February or March. Divide the old crowns into roots each bearing a single crown or eye, and plant these in the same way as shown above.

Harvesting Do not pull any sticks the first year, and only a moderate amount the second year. Keep the beds free from weeds, well watered, and mulched with compost. Feed with Maxicrop during the summer and give a dressing of fish manure at the rate of 4–5 oz per square yard after the last pulling at the end of July.

Forcing Roots may be taken up a brought into a warm dark place for forcing from December onwards. Place in a deep box, cover roots with light soil and keep moist. Plants outside may be hastened on by covering with straw or leaves and a box, tub or whitewashed cloche placed over them.

Varieties *Champagne Early.* An outstandingly good variety, comes true from seed. *Prince Albert.* Good for forcing. *Victoria.* Comes true from seed. *Holstein Bloodred.* A vigorous grower, producing blood-red stalks.

The keen vegetable gardener should aim to produce crops suitable for salad purposes all the year round. This can only be done if he is prepared to grow some of the more unusual plants, or to use in salads vegetables normally thought of as only fit for 'boiling'.

The great advantage of eating vegetables raw is concerned largely with their vitamin content. Fresh vegetables, used straight from the garden, contain far more vitamins than those that are cooked or even fresh ones from the shops, because serious vitamin losses occur during travel. Lettuce, too, in many cases, provides the vitamins so necessary for human diet. Some plants – it may be the stems or the leaves – have to be blanched before they are consumable, while others can be eaten just as they grow.

The following are the principal salad crops:

Beetroot

When this crop is used as a salad, the roots should be pulled before they become coarse, and may be either used immediately or may be stored for use during the winter months.

Celeriac

The method of growing this vegetable is described in Chapter 7. It can be used in salads.

Celery

A very popular salad, both the self-blanching celery, which comes in early, and the main crop celery, which is useful in November, December and January.

Chervil

Chervil is described as a herb, but small quantities may be used to flavour salads.

Chicory

Plants may be raised if seed is sown on well-prepared land early in June in rows 18 ins apart. When the seedlings are through thin them to 1 ft apart. When growing, chicory resembles the dandelion. Hoe regularly, and in November dig up the roots and place them in boxes of sand tightly against the other. The boxes may then be taken and placed for forcing, also under the staging of the greenhouse providing this is kept dark, or under whitewashed cloches with the soil heated below by an electric warming unit. The yellow leaves thus produced are most tender, and may be in use from October to May providing successional 'forcings' are made. The best variety to grow is the Witloof.

Chives

These prove a very useful crop, and make it possible to have the subtle onion flavouring all the year round. The plants make a nice edging to a border, and grow well under quite dry conditions. The plants may be propagated by division in the spring. Planted 1 ft apart.

Corn Salad

A salad crop much neglected but which comes in very useful from Christmas onwards. Sow the seeds in rows 1 ft apart in September, and thin out the plants when large enough, to 6 ins apart. The leaves of the corn salad resemble the forget-me-not. Gathered one at a time from the plants and wash before using. Some people prefer the round-leaved variety, while others like the Regence.

Cucumber

During the summer it is possible to have cucumbers growing out of doors; and home grown ones are welcomed. Ridge varieties may be grown.

Soil Cucumbers like a soil rich in organic matter, moist but well drained.

Preparation of Soil Prepare the soil in such a way that there is a 3in layer of well-rotted vegetable refuse 4 ins down. Dig a hole where the plant is to grow, making it half a spade in depth and a spade wide. After putting the rotting material at the bottom replace the soil to form a mound.

Seed Sowing The seeds may be sown in the glasshouse in early April and then planted out under cloches in early May; or sown at the end of April and planted out of doors at the end of May, or beginning of June, when fear of frost is over. Seeds may be sown in a prepared seedbed as advised for tomatoes, the seeds being placed 3 ins apart and $\frac{1}{2}$ in deep; or sown on prepared mounds under upturned glass jam-jars.

Planting Out When the seedlings have made their first pair of true leaves they should be planted out in the positions where they are to grow – 3 ft apart.

Stopping and Pollinating Nip out the top of Ridge cucumbers when seven leaves have formed – this is all the stopping that is necessary. Retain the male blooms as these are necessary for a good set of fruit.

Watering and Feeding It is usually necessary to water three times a week during hot weather. Cucumbers like moist conditions and these help to keep down the red spider. The ends of the cloches may be removed in day time, and the tops flecked over with a little limewash, to break up the sun's rays and give a little shade. When the first fruits are about 3 ins long, water every five days with liquid manure.

Harvesting Cut the cucumbers as desired but never let them get too old. Keep cutting when they are a good size and the plants will keep cropping. It is possible to get 40 good cucumbers from a Ridge variety.

General Remarks As cucumbers are surfacing they should be given a good mulch of well-rotted compost or peat. Be sure not to expose the roots by washing the soil off when watering nor let water collect round the stems as this may cause stem rot.

Varieties *King of the Ridge.* The best of all Ridge types. Large cucumbers; plants crop heavily; fruits almost spineless. *Conqueror.* The best of the Frame varieties for frame or cloche work. *Burpee Hybrid.* The best outdoor cucumber, a heavy cropper of 9–12 ins, straight and well formed fruits, smooth-skinned and very dark green. *Burpless.* An outdoor cucumber which can be grown like the ordinary Ridge varieties. Early and very productive, the dark green fruits 10–12 ins long; not bitter or indigestible; the skin is tender and soft and peeling is unnecessary.

Dandelion

The cultivated dandelion is grown in a similar manner to chicory. It grows well on dry soils, and there is no need to give it any special manuring. Sow the seeds in May in rows 1 ft apart, and thin plant to 1 ft apart. From November onwards the roots are lifted and forced, as for seakale. They can also be covered with forcing-pots and blanched where they are to grow after the turn of the year. This blanching is necessary as the green leaves are rather bitter. It is possible to force roots in boxes, or under cloches as advised for Chicory.

Endive

A salad much used on the Continent, and becoming increasingly popular in the USA. The main sowing should be made in a moist border in June or July, in rows 1 ft apart. The seed is slow to germinate and the seedlings slow to grow. Water regularly to encourage growth. When the plants are fit to handle they may be transferred and planted out just as cabbage lettuce. Grown in the same way as lettuce. Endive should, however, be blanched, and this is done in various ways: (1) the outer leaves are tied up over the heart; (2) a large flower-pot is inverted over each plant; (3) a slate is laid on top of the plant instead, and (4) the plants are taken up bodily and planted in soil in a dark shed for a fortnight to bleach.

Much the easiest way of blanching endive is to white-wash the inside of one or two cloches and then to stand these over the plants – closing up the ends of the short row thus made with a square of wood or a sheet of whitewashed glass. The plants are thus kept from the light; not 'squashed' and yet grown with perfect ventilation. The result is they are excellent to eat in three weeks' time.

Varieties : *Moss Curled.* Leaves are crinkly and crisp. *Batavian.* Leaves more like a lettuce.

Lettuce

There is no need to extol the excellence of this crop, as it forms the basis of most salads.

Mint

Mint, though not usually thought of as a salad, may be incorporated if it is chopped up fine or used in quite small quantities. It gives that 'unusual flavour'.

Mustard and Cress

This would seem to be one of the most easily grown crops, and yet on certain soils it 'damps off' easily. For this reason the seed may be sown on damped fine sedge peat, firmed in boxes.

Sow cress three days before the mustard seed, and keep the boxes in the dark. It is usually convenient to sow in boxes, and these may be kept in the dark for a few days to ensure long stems. Remove from dark five days before cutting, to get the green colouring-matter back into the leaves. Cut with scissors when required, as to pull them up by the roots is apt to make the salad gritty.

The best variety for sowing is the white mustard. After the middle of March, mustard and cress may be sown outside, first of all in the south border and then in the north border. Successive sowings may be made until the middle of September.

Nasturtium

Few people think of nasturtiums as a salad plant, though the flowers are often used for garnishing. Actually the flowers can be eaten, and the seeds which form subsequently can be included in salads also, though they are somewhat 'hot'. Nasturtiums will grow well in any poor soil.

Carters

**Carrot
Early Nantes**

Unwins

**Continuity
When cutting brussels sprouts, leave
a short stalk**

Unwins

**Green Sleeves
Protect celery in a hard winter
with straw or bracken**

Unwins

**Histon Cropper
Soil for tomatoes must be
deeply worked**

Onion

A large number of types are described in this book. It is not necessary to use large quantities of this crop in a salad, as just a 'wipe round the bowl' with chives, for instance, is sufficient to give a piquant flavour.

Parsley

Like mint, this is more generally used for garnishing and for flavouring. It is, however, a useful adjunct to any salad, providing it is used intelligently.

Radish

This crop is much liked, not only because of the colour it gives to a salad, but because of its flavour. Radishes should not only be pulled young, but when they are crisp and fresh. There are many different varieties.

Rampion

The roots may be used for salads, fresh or cooked.

Sorrel

Sorrel may either be used for a salad or cooked with spinach. It grows best on a light loam, and the seeds should be sown early in April in shallow drills 18 ins apart. The seedlings should be thinned early, leaving 3 ins between the plants in the rows. Hoe the bed to keep it free from weeds. If necessary, all the plants may be transplanted to another piece of ground, allowing 18 ins between each plant. Thin the plants growing on the original patch to that distance. Directly any flowering stems appear, they should be pinched out. The leaves should be picked off as required, and the younger and fresher they are the better are they suited for the salad-bowl.

Tomatoes

More and more amateurs are growing tomatoes outside and are finding them comparatively easy to grow.

9 Herb Culture

Although not used as foods, herbs can make a great deal of difference to the tastiness of a dish. Their aroma and flavour are their chief values. Herbs are no longer grown extensively, but they are worthy of a modest place in your vegetable garden. Mint, parsley, sage and thyme are probably the most popular. In pots and tubs, herbs also make attractive container plants.

Balm

This is one of the easiest of all the herbs to grow. It is a perennial, and can be propagated by cuttings or grown as an annual from seed. The plant is herbaceous, and bears crinkled circular leaves. The seed may be sown in May; cuttings may also be taken in May.

Basil

There are two forms of Basil, the most popular of which is sweet basil. Sow the seeds in February or March, in heat, and plant the seedlings out in May in rows 12 ins apart, the plants 8 ins in the rows. When the plants are in flower cut and dry the shoots to the ground. Some growers lift the plants in September and pot them, in order to obtain fresh green leaves throughout the winter. Bush Basil may be sown outside in April.

Borage

This is always an interesting herb to grow, because it has a great attraction for bees. It grows well on poor soil, while the flowers and leaves are very popular for flavouring purposes. It is a rampant spreading grower. In cider and claret cup, two or three borage leaves impart a delicious flavour.

The plant normally grows 18 ins high with bristly leaves 3 ins long. The flowers are bright blue. Sow the seed in April or early May in rows 2 ft apart, and thin the plants 18 ins apart. It is possible to propagate also by division from cuttings of the old stock.

Caraway

Caraway seeds are used for flavouring cakes, etc. The root of the caraway is also edible. It looks and tastes something like a carrot. The leaves and shoots of this plant can be used for salads. The plant grows 12 to 15 ins high, and the seed is sown in May or early June in rows 18 ins apart. Thin the plants 6 ins apart. The seeds should be ready for gathering in September.

Chervil

Use Chervil fresh for flavouring soups and salads. It is often used for garnishing instead of parsley. For this purpose the curled chervil is most suitable. Seed should be sown any time from July to October in drills 10 ins apart and thin the seedlings so they are 6 ins apart. Fresh seed is essential. During a hot summer water the plants frequently to prevent them from going to seed. Pick off the leaves as required.

Fennel

A hardy perennial which produces a quantity of feathery foliage, used either for garnishing or for fish sauces. It is possible to blanch the stems and use them like celery. The seeds, when saved, may be used for flavouring also. There are many kinds of fennel, but it is the garden fennel that is grown in this country. Sow the seed in the south in mid-April, and in the north in early May. The drills may be 18 ins apart and the seedlings thinned to 6-8 ins apart. If the stems are required for culinary purposes, they should be earthed up when the base begins to swell. They are usually blanched ten days afterwards and are then ready for use.

Marjoram

There are several kinds of Marjoram, two of which are grown in private gardens, the Sweet Marjoram and the Pot Marjoram. The Pot Marjoram has more branches, violet flowers, and a reddish tinge suffuses the plants. The sweet marjoram makes a bushy plant which bears white flowers in June and July. The leaves of the Pot Marjoram and Sweet Marjoram are used green, and, when dried, for flavouring. The latter is said to be a tonic.

Sow the seeds out of doors in April in rows 1 ft apart. Thin the plants in the case of the pot marjoram to 9 ins apart and sweet marjoram 6 ins apart.

Mint

There are many kinds of mint, the Peppermint, Spearmint, *Mentha longifolia, Mentha rotundifolia,* etc. The Spearmint is the variety which is most used for mint sauce. It is hardy but susceptible to mint rust. Some epicures prefer Mentha rotundifolia (the apple mint) because of its flavour, while others dislike its hairiness. All mints are propagated by means of the division of roots, and in order to obtain fresh young green leaves throughout the year the roots are often forced during the months of November to May. This forcing is quite easy to carry out if the roots are chopped up into pieces an inch long and packed tightly in a seed bed, and covered above and below with an inch or so of soil. It is possible also to cut stems in the autumn and hang them up in a cool place to dry, ready for use during the winter and spring.

A damp situation suits mint best, and in order to keep it free from rust a new situation should be made every year early in March. In cases where the rust is very bad, the roots should be washed before planting out and put in warm water at 110 degrees F for twenty minutes. The washing alone may remove the rust spores, and thoroughly washed material usually grows free from rust the following year. After washing, the underground stems should be trimmed so as to remove the above-ground parts.

Parsley

For good results, Parsley should always be sown thinly. Thinning should always be done early to prevent the plants from crowding one another.

Parsley makes a very good edging plant, and prefers a deep rich, moist soil, though I have seen it growing as well in a clayey soil as in sand.

The principal sowings of parsley may be made in March for the summer and June for the winter; if one sowing is made, this should be done in May. Those with a glasshouse can make a sowing in heat in February, and, after pricking, the young plants thus raised out into further boxes, they may be transplanted further in rows 1 ft apart, the plants being 1 ft apart also.

Sow the seed in rows 1 ft apart. They should be thinned in the first place to 3 ins and finally to 6 ins. These thinnings may be transplanted to other rows if necessary.

With the aid of a cloche or two it is possible to have plenty of parsley all the year round outside. The cutting down of plants when fully grown generally defers flowering and seeding which does so much harm to future cropping. It is possible to pot up the best plants at the end of September and take them into a cool greenhouse.

VARIETIES *New Dark Green Winter.* A very compact grower which produces emerald green leaves which stand the winter well. *King of the Parsleys.* A heavy cropper, dwarf curled. *Champion Moss Curled.* Produces a very dark-green tightly curled leaf.

Radish, Horse

This is a very popular condiment with roast beef. It can become a nuisance in the garden if not correctly grown, as it spreads like a weed.

The best way to grow it is to make a little mound in December 2 ft high and 2 ft wide and as long as desired, and to see that this mound is on well-firmed soil – a path, or even concrete. Young roots about ½ in in diameter may then be cut 9 ins in length, and may be laid in sand until March. At this time of the year the majority of them will have sprouted, so plant the best in the mound 12 ins apart and 18 ins from the normal level of the soil. The thongs should be inserted pointing downwards.

If the mound is made of good soil, a good, long, thick, straight root will form which can easily be stored in sand in winter.

To uncover the horse radish the mound can be razed to the ground and the roots thus exposed. The advantage of the mound method is that it is impossible for the roots to spread throughout the soil, and it ensures good thick sticks being produced.

Sage

Sage is a popular herb, being used as a seasoning with duck, sausages, or even with cheeses. There are two main sages, the Green Sage and the Red Sage. The green sage has wrinkled, velvety leaves and grows like a little shrub. Red sage has violet-coloured leaves and is not very popular.

When purchasing plants of the green sage, it is advisable to ask for the broad-leaved green, as this is regarded as the better type. It is better to buy plants than to sow seed, as seedlings can never be fully relied on. Cuttings may be taken with a heel in April or May, and may be rooted in a sandy medium. They will generally root quickly in frames, but they will grow quite well in the open ground.

The plants thus raised should be planted out in rows 2 ft apart, each plant being 1 ft apart. After planting they should be regularly hoed, and when plants show signs of flower the flowering stem should be cut back. Take cuttings, and renew the sage row once every four years.

Savory

This has a very strong flavour, and should be used in a similar manner to thyme. The summer savory should be raised annually from seed, while the winter savory is a perennial usually propagated by cuttings. When growing it looks rather like rosemary. Both of them are cut when the stems are in full flower and tied up in bunches to dry for winter use.

It is possible to raise both kinds from seeds sown in April in drills 1 ft apart. Thin the seedlings to 6 ins apart.

Tarragon

This is mainly used for flavouring vinegar, but it is also useful in salads and flavouring omelettes.

The plant is a perennial which grows like a bush 4 ft high, bears slender shoots and thin, delicate textured leaves. The fresh herb has to be used, as the oil of tarragon disappears when the herb is dried.

The plants should be put out in a well-drained sheltered situation 2 ft square. It is quite easy to propagate by means of division or by cuttings, which should be struck in frames or in gentle heat in the spring.

As in the case of parsley, it is possible to dig up one or two plants and winter them in cold frames to keep up a continuous supply of fresh green leaves.

Thyme

This is a useful herb for flavouring stews and soups and is the best adjunct to jugged hare. There are two main types, the Common Thyme and the Lemon Thyme. The latter can only be propagated by the division of roots in March and April, or by cuttings in September, while the former can be raised from seed sown in the spring, although the division of roots is preferable.

Thyme may be used as an effective edging or in dry borders where parsley will not grow readily.

It is necessary to ensure frequent division or the plants become leggy and may die out. The rows should be 2 ft apart and the plants 18 ins apart.

In exposed situations and under northern conditions it may be necessary to earth the plants up in order to give them some protection throughout the winter. Under such conditions growth may be encouraged by the application of potassic nitrate of soda at the rate of 1 oz to the yard run, in spring.

It is impossible to keep vegetables entirely free from pests and diseases. The number that might attack a crop is count-less. Here is a list of those that in my experience are the most common in the gardens of this country, with details of the controls I recommend to tackle them successfully.

PESTS THAT ATTACK MANY VEGETABLES

Certain pests attack various kinds of vegetables. I consider it better to list these first of all, before dealing with each individual crop.

APHIDES   Sometimes known as green fly, blue bug, black fly, etc. A very large family of plant lice which will attack all members of the cabbage family as well as beans, peas, carrots, etc. These sucking insects usually attack the under surface of the leaf first of all. They cause the leaves to curl in many cases, and for this reason they are often difficult to get at with a spray or dust. Because they multiply at an extra-ordinary rate, they should be controlled in the early stages.
CONTROL   Derris should be applied either as a dust or as a spray. In the case of badly curled leaves, a nicotine spray may be necessary, so that the fumes may penetrate to the insects. Derris is safe to use at any time, as it is not poisonous to man.

BEETLES, FLEA   Flea beetles are small, and generally black or dark grey. They damage young plants when they are coming through, particularly in the case of cabbages, turnips and radishes, but they will attack the leaves of larger plants also. They can generally be recognized because they hop quickly and hide themselves. Large numbers of them on a plant may cause it to look quite black. They spend the winter in dry vegetable rubbish such as is found in hedge-bottoms, and may commence attacking plants in May and continue right on into August.
CONTROL   Where this pest is common the seeds of all the cabbage family should be well wetted with turpentine, using it at the rate of $\frac{1}{8}$-pint to $\frac{1}{2}$-lb seed. The seed should be then dried overnight and sown the next day. Just before the plants are through, a good dusting may be given with Derris and Pyrethrum dust, as it is in this stage that the beetles often do the greatest harm. Further dustings may be neces-sary at weekly intervals until the plants are quite free.

CATERPILLARS   Different kinds of caterpillars may be found on vegetables, but most commonly on the cabbage family.
CONTROL   They are easy to control by spraying with strong Derris liquid.

CATERPILLARS, SURFACE   Surface caterpillars wander about just above and below the surface of the ground and damage plants by biting through their stems. Some caterpillars are $1\frac{1}{2}$ ins long and some only $\frac{1}{2}$ in long, and they are usually brown or grey in colour. They feed at night, and during the day they hide under clods of earth or stones.
CONTROL   Hoe the land regularly, especially during the months of July and August to prevent egg-laying from taking place. Regular hoeing will also destroy the young larvae.

LEATHER-JACKETS   This is the young of the Daddy-longlegs. It is generally about $1\frac{1}{2}$ins long, greyish-brown in colour, and has no legs. The skin of the grub is very tough. Leather-jackets live 1-2 ins below the surface of the soil, and so are able to feed on the stems and roots of plants below ground. At night they surface and eat the leaves. Sometimes they pull these down into the ground.
CONTROL   Bran should be applied all over the surface of the ground with a further application the following day if necessary. Leather-jackets are particularly fond of bran, and will come up to feed. The birds will then eat them.

MILLIPEDES   Millipedes may do a great deal of harm to the roots and stems of plants underground. They have round bodies which, when young, are $\frac{1}{2}$in long, and as they grow older 1 in long. The front four segments of their bodies have a pair of legs each, while the remaining segments have two pairs of legs. They should never be confused with centipedes, which are carnivorous and do a great deal of good in destroying other pests. Centipedes have flattened bodies, and each segment of the body has only one pair of legs.
CONTROL   Napthalene should be forked into the soil at the rate of 1 oz to the square yard. This may act as a deterrent. Large numbers may be trapped if a large carrot is cut into two pieces longitudinally and buried an inch or two below

the ground. If these pieces are spitted on a stick they may easily be removed, and the millipedes that have collected may be extracted and destroyed.

SLUGS   Slugs do a great deal of damage in the vegetable garden, not only to members of the cabbage family but to potatoes, celery and so on. They feed above the ground during the night, and below ground at any time. They do not like frost or dry soil, and so burrow down deeply into the ground when these conditions occur. They often lay eggs in batches of 4–50 (depending on the type of slug), in damp soil or under stones. The eggs can be recognized because they are white, translucent and glistening. They usually turn yellow and opaque as the embryo starts to grow. Hatching will usually take place in a month.
CONTROL   When sedge peat or compost is used as a mulch all over the ground slugs cannot move about and so die.

WIREWORM   Unfortunately, this insect, which is really the grub of the click beetle, may live in the soil for 6–7 years before turning into a beetle. Wireworms, like millipedes, damage plants below ground.
CONTROL   Cut carrots in half lengthways. Spit them on a 3ft bamboo. Bury the cut carrots 1in deep in the soil. After a week, pull out the root and kill the wireworms that have burrowed in. Re-bury the carrot again for another "catch".
   Alternatively, sow mustard seed thickly all over the affected land. The mustard may be broken up with a fork 8 weeks later, sprinkled with fish manure at 3 oz per square yard and then lightly dug in.

Asparagus

ASPARAGUS BEETLE   This beetle is very easy to recognize, as it has a black and red body with black and yellow wing cases. The small larvae will be found on the leaves of the asparagus during the summer, eating the foliage. In the winter the beetles hide amongst rubbish.
CONTROL   The foliage should be cut down directly it starts to turn yellow in the autumn, and burnt. The beds should be sprayed with nicotine and soft soap during the summer if the beetles are seen.

Cabbage

APHIS, MEALY CABBAGE   This is a mealy mauve-coloured aphis which attacks the under surface of the leaves of the plants. It is a great nuisance in the case of Brussels sprouts as it gets into the sprouts themselves.

CONTROL   Spray or dust with nicotine or use Derris. They often live on the old Brussels sprouts throughout the winter, and so directly the crop has been cleared the old stumps should be taken up.

CABBAGE ROOT FLY   The maggots will be found on the stem of the plant just below ground level, and the larvae burrow down and attack the plants. These should not be confused with the turnip gall weevil, which makes a blister and is seen in the autumn.

CONTROL   Cut square discs, 3 ins by 3 ins, out of tarred felt. Then, after cutting a slit in the middle of one side to the centre of the disc, slip the disc around the base of the stem of the plant so that it lies flat on top of the soil. The flies will be unable to reach the roots to lay their eggs. It is these eggs, of course, that hatch out into maggots.

CABBAGE WHITE FLY   Tiny white waxy flies may be found on the under surface of leaves. They suck the sap and make the plants unpalatable because of the mess they leave behind.

CONTROL   As for aphis.

CATERPILLARS   These are the larvae of the white butterfly which may be found flitting about the cabbage bed. Eggs are laid in large numbers, and the caterpillars soon eat the leaves.

CONTROL   Spray with liquid Derris. In small gardens hand-picking is possible. It should be remembered that a fungus causing plant disease is a plant growing on another plant.

CLUB ROOT   This disease is one of the commonest in the country today. The cabbage may wilt on hot sunny days and recover in the evening. When the root system is examined, the large swelling characteristic of this disease will be found to have turned into a club-like mass. The spores of this disease can remain in the soil for many years.

CONTROL   In the first place, the soil should be well limed, as the club root disease is always worse on acid soils. Hydrated lime should be applied to the surface of the soil at 7 or 8 oz to the square yard during the month of January. Generally, the infection takes place in the seedbed, though when the plants are put out they seldom appear obviously clubbed. For this reason few growers realize that the plants are already diseased. Recently it has been discovered that if crushed egg-shells are mixed with wood ashes on a 50–50 basis they will help to control club root. Half a handful of this mixture is put in the holes at planting time. It is known that club root dislikes lime, and the lime in egg shells appears to be even more effective than hydrated lime.

Carrots

CARROT FLY   A small shiny bottle-green fly. It lays its eggs near the surface of the ground along carrot rows. The larvae then burrow down to the base of the root and tunnel into it. Large numbers of maggots may be found in attacked roots. CONTROL   Whizzed napthalene applied between the rows at 1 oz to the yard run creates a smell which usually keeps the carrot fly away. Growing onions and carrots in alternate rows mystifies the pests as a rule and so neither crop is attacked. The variety known as *Autumn King* is very resistant to the attacks of carrot fly maggots.

See Cabbage.

Celery

CELERY FLY   The female lays her eggs on the under sides of the leaves, and the maggots that hatch out then make their way in between the upper and lower epidermis of the leaves. In this way whitish-looking blisters are formed. In the early stages these may be picked off.
CONTROL   See that the young plants are free from the pest by spraying regularly with nicotine and soft soap. When in the trenches, a regular soaking with the same spray is necessary early in June to control the second generation. A third generation may appear in September. Experiments have shown that a repellant consiting of one part of creosote to 99 parts by weight of precipitated chalk has proved useful. This dust is scattered among the plants thinly, and the creosote smell keeps the flies away.
LEAF SPOT (OR 'BLIGHT')   Celery leaves turn brown in patches, and little black spots may appear on them. The leaf stalks may also be attacked. If the disease is not controlled, the whole leaf may wither away and the plants can thus be ruined. The disease is generally first seen in July.
CONTROL   The plants should be sprayed three times from the end of June (*i.e.* once a fortnight) with Bordeaux mixture, to cover the upper and lower surface of the leaves. In

very wet years, four or five further applications may be advisable. Ask your seeds merchant for a guarantee that the seeds supplied have been treated with the correct solution of formaldehyde.

Mint

MINT RUST   Little orange cushions may be seen on the leaves and stems of the plants. In the case of a bad attack, the shoots become thickened in a peculiar manner, the leaves are much smaller, and may be distorted.

CONTROL   Early in October, the mint tops should be burnt off where they are growing by laying down dry straw on the mint bed and burning, so causing a rapid fire. A fire of this kind should not injure the roots and yet burns up the stems and kills the disease spores.

Onions

ONION FLY   This is one of the worst pests that a garden has to endure, and yet it is now one of the easiest to control. The female of the onion fly, which is rather like a small house fly, lays her eggs either on the neck of the onion or at soil level. The larvae which hatch out burrow to the bottom of the bulb and feed. The first attack usually takes place some time in May. Growing carrots and onions in alternate rows usually 'foxes' the flies and they keep away. The smell of the one vegetable keeps away the pest of the other.

CONTROL   Apply whizzed napthalene along the rows at the rate of 1 oz to the yard run just before thinning, and again ten days later. When hoeing among onions, great care should be taken to see that the plants are never damaged, as the odour that attracts the insects is then given off.

DOWNY-MILDEW   A greyish-white mildew may be seen on the leaves, and soon afterwards these turn yellow and collapse completely.

CONTROL   The dusting of the rows with fine sulphur dust at the rate of 3 to 4 oz to the yard run has given good results. The autumn and spring-sown crops should be kept well apart, as this prevents the infection passing from one to the other.

Parsnips

CANKER   The roots of parsnips may appear cracked. Brown rot then sets in, and soon after, a wet rot destroys the root completely.

CONTROL   Though included in this chapter as a disease,

most mycologists do not believe that this trouble is due to any specific parasite. Avon Resister is fairly resistant variety.

Peas

PEA MOTH   The moths lay their eggs on the pods and the larvae burrow in and destroy the peas. Several maggots may be found in a pod.

CONTROL   Spray the plants with nicotine just as the flowers are setting. In this way the larvae may be killed as they are tunnelling in. As the larvae drop to the ground when full grown, the soil should be cultivated continually so that they may be destroyed.

PEA AND BEAN WEEVILS   The weevil eats peculiar semi-circular holes out of the sides of the leaves and often does a great deal of harm when the plants are young.

CONTROL   Dust with Derris early in the morning or late in the day. Hoe regularly between the rows to destroy the clods, the weevils' hiding places.

PEA AND BEAN THRIPS   One of the most serious pests of peas in some districts. Thrips are tiny black flies, and are difficult to detect unless the plants are shaken and the thrips are made to fall on to a white handkerchief. They attack seedlings, suck the sap from growing points, and so distort plants and prevent them from growing healthily. They are generally worse in a dry season. Thrip-attacked pods look silver to start with, but later turn brown.

CONTROL   See that the soil is limed at the rate of 4 oz to the square yard when the seed is sown. When the majority of the flowers have set, spray with nicotine and soft soap.

MILDEW   The leaves, the stems, and the pods are found to be covered with a white powdery substance. This trouble usually appears on the later sown varieties and towards the end of the summer.

CONTROL   The plants should be well dusted with a good sulphur dust early in the morning, while the dew is still on them.

Potato

POTATO BLIGHT   The leaves of the potatoes are attacked by this disease, and dark green spots or blotches of irregular sizes and shapes appear. These turn brown or almost black. The disease may spread at an alarming rate. The spores fall on the ground and thus may infect the new tubers. Dark sunken areas appear on the skin, and the potatoes become rotten and useless.

CONTROL   The disease may be controlled by Bordeaux or Burgundy. Burgundy is easy to prepare and is as effective as Bordeaux. Note its preparation below:

Crush 2½ pounds of washing soda into a 2½ gallon bucket of cold water, and stir until fully dissolved. Place 2 pounds of powdered copper sulphate into a wooden tub containing 17 gallons of water, stir and leave overnight. Pour washing soda solution into this tub the next morning and stir vigorously. The plants may then be sprayed with the solution.

Those who have no facilities for mixing washes may buy colloidal copper sprays already prepared.

COMMON SCAB   Common Scab affects potatoes, and causes brown corky scabs to appear on the tubers. The tuber in consequence has to be more deeply peeled and a good deal of potato is wasted.

CONTROL   The shallow furrows where the potatoes are to grow should be filled with fresh grass mowings.

Spinach

MILDEW   The leaves of spinach are sometimes covered with yellow spots, the undersides of which will be found to be covered with a violet or grey mould.

CONTROL   The plants should be dusted from time to time with a good sulphur dust; this must be done in the earliest stages.

Tomatoes

POTATO BLIGHT   Attacks tomatoes very badly – devastates them in a week or so if not prevented or controlled.

CONTROL   Spray with Bordeaux or Burgundy Mixture as for potatoes, or dust with a copper-lime dust.

Index